THE CHRISTMAS STORY, RETOLD

Warren Ravenscroft

ISBN: 979-8-88525-716-9 (paperback)

Edited by Beverley Bartlett Ravenscroft and Phil Gutteridge

Cover art by Aaron Pocock

Published in Australia by Warren Ravenscroft.
www.wittonbooks.com

A catalogue record for this
book is available from the
National Library of Australia

Contents

Introduction

Our understanding of the Nativity story has been distorted over the years as new Christmas traditions have developed. Many of these interpretations are now taken as fact. With an in-depth study of the original texts as described in the Gospels, and the facts laid out in order, a very different Nativity emerges from the one celebrated in many churches today. For this reason, under the guidance of the Holy Spirit, I have written an allegory, to represent the Nativity as presented in the Gospels, hidden by a misconception. While most versions of the Nativity contain an element of truth, uncovering truth recorded in the Biblical accounts reveals the real Jesus Christ, and Father God is glorified.

Part One

The Christmas Story, Retold

The 'Day of Preparation' had arrived in the busy town of Nazareth. Mary was completing tasks, making ready those requirements for the evening meal shared with her parents and Salome. Suddenly she was aware of another person in the room. She turned, eager to see who had visited her.

As she looked around, Mary saw a heavenly being. He greeted Mary, "Rejoice highly favoured one, the Lord is with you; blessed are you among women!"

Mary was afraid and shrunk back. The Angel introduced himself as Gabriel, and continued, *"Do not be afraid, Mary, for you have found favour with God. You will conceive in your womb and bring forth a Son, and shall call His name Jesus. He will be great, and will be called the Son of the Highest; and the Lord God will give Him the throne of His father David. He will reign over the house of Jacob forever, and of His kingdom there will be no end."*

Mary wondered what the angel's message meant. She was betrothed to Joseph who was at his parent's home, building a room for them both to live in once they were married. Being with a child before the official marriage ceremony to Joseph could mean certain death for her. In trepidation, she whispered, "But how can what God ordained be possible, as I am engaged to Joseph?"

Gabriel nodded knowingly and replied, *"The Holy Spirit will come upon you, and the power of the Highest will overshadow you; the Holy One to be born will be called the Son of God. Remember your Aunt Elizabeth has also conceived a son in her old age; and this is now the sixth month for she who was called barren. Remember, with God, nothing will be impossible."*

Mary slowly processed everything the Angel said, and replied, *"Behold the maidservant of the Lord! Let it be to me according to your word."* In an instant, the angel was gone.

When the family gathered for the evening Passover meal, Mary shared everything that had happened with her parents.

"Abba, Mother, I need to talk to you. I really don't know how to explain what happened today, it all seems so strange. While I was baking bread, I felt a strange presence in the house. I was visited by an Angelic being. He told me his name was Gabriel and that I am going to become pregnant by the Holy Spirit, not by Joseph. What am I supposed to do? I am sure this is a message from God, and I need to obey God's instructions, but what if people don't believe me? I will be stoned to death and we will all be disgraced," said Mary.

"My daughter, Mary, what else did the angel say to you?" replied Heli, her father, in a voice that contained so much concern.

Mary continued, "He mentioned Aunt Elizabeth and her pregnancy and said that nothing is impossible to God."

There was silence for what seemed like an eternity, then Heli looked at his wife and said, "Maybe it would be good for Mary to travel to Jerusalem and be a help to your sister? As we know, she is of an age where the household duties, and being with child, would be quite a strain on her."

"I think that is a wonderful idea. Salome is quite capable of completing the home duties here," replied Mary's mother.

"I would be able to talk with Aunt Elizabeth about their encounter with the Angel Gabriel. Uncle Zacharias would be free to continue his temple duties without concern for his wife. Perhaps they can help us all understand what the angel has told us concerning me?" said Mary.

And so it was that Mary packed some clothes and food and left Nazareth for the four-day journey to Jerusalem and the home of Zacharias and Elizabeth.

When Mary arrived at the home in Jerusalem, Elizabeth was filled with joy. She wrapped her arms around her niece and greeted her with a kiss on each cheek.

"Aunt Elizabeth," said Mary, resting her head on Elizabeth's shoulder.

"Mary, how delightful to see you. What bought you all this way to see us?" replied Elizabeth.

"Aunt Elizabeth we were overjoyed at your miraculous news of the forthcoming birth of your child," said Mary.

Mary continued, "Abba and Mother thought I should visit you because you may need some help and I need some answers."

Elizabeth indicated a pile of cushions and the two sat down side by side, as Elizabeth held Mary's hand.

"Oh, my child, whatever is the matter? Has something happened between you and Joseph?" asked Elizabeth.

"Dearest Aunt, I hardly know how to explain. I had a visit by the angel Gabriel. He told me I am going to have a child by the Holy Spirit," replied Mary. When Elizabeth heard this, the baby in her womb jumped for joy.

"Did you see what just happened, Mary? My baby jumped for joy in my womb," Elizabeth replied in excitement.

Elizabeth burst into prophecy over Mary. *"Blessed are you among women, and blessed is the fruit of your womb!"* Elizabeth focused her eyes on Mary and said, "But why is this granted to me, that the mother of my Lord should come to me?" Elizabeth again burst into prophecy, *"Blessed is she who believed, for there will be fulfilment of those things which were told you from the Lord,"* stated Elizabeth.

When Zacharias returned home from his temple duties, Elizabeth rushed to meet him with his writing tablet in her hand. She wrote, "Our niece Mary has been chosen by our Lord to be the mother of the Messiah."

Zacharias, a Levite priest, didn't say anything. He had been struck mute when the angel Gabriel appeared and told him his barren wife Elizabeth would bear a child. Elizabeth noticed Zacharias was concerned about his niece. Elizabeth said, "My dear niece, come and sit here and tell us everything the Angel told you." Zacharias beckoned Mary to sit near him. And so, Mary shared every minute detail with them both, as Elizabeth wrote on the tablet.

Over the next weeks, Mary helped with the household chores and attended to her Aunt Elizabeth. Zacharias was able to attend to his temple duties, without the concern for his wife. I am sure Elizabeth and Mary would have spent much time in discussion and prayer during Mary's three-month long stay.

As time passed for Mary, and, feeling encouraged by her visit with her Aunt, she burst into a song of praise to glorify God.

"My soul magnifies the Lord,
And my spirit has rejoiced in God my Saviour.

For He has regarded the lowly state of His maidservant;
For behold, henceforth all generations will call me blessed.
For He who is mighty has done great things for me,
And holy is His name.
And His mercy is on those who fear Him
From generation to generation.
He has shown strength with His arm;
He has scattered the proud in the imagination of their hearts.
He has put down the mighty from their thrones,
And exalted the lowly.
He has filled the hungry with good things,
And the rich He has sent away empty.
He has helped His servant Israel,
In remembrance of His mercy,
As He spoke to our fathers,
To Abraham and to his seed forever."

It wasn't long before Elizabeth gave birth to her son. Mary, with the other relatives and neighbours were also excited for the couple and at the way the Lord had shown great mercy to them both. After eight days, those chosen came to circumcise the child. The child would also be named, some suggesting the baby be called Zacharias after his father, but Elizabeth objected.

"No! His name is John," she replied adamantly.

"But you don't have anyone in your family by that name. What do you mean, John?" replied those who were performing the circumcision. Not taking any notice of Elizabeth, they went to Zacharias and made signs to him to inquire what the baby was to be called. To their amazement, he took a writing tablet and wrote, "His name is John!" Immediately, Zacharias was able to speak and hear again. Those in attendance and also those who heard throughout the hill country of Judea, discussed all that had happened, wondering within themselves saying, "What kind of child will this be?"

Zacharias was filled with the Holy Spirit, and he prophesied saying:

"Blessed is the Lord God of Israel,
For He has visited and redeemed His people,
And has raised up a horn of salvation for us
In the house of His servant David,
As He spoke by the mouth of His holy prophets,
Who have been since the world began,
That we should be saved from our enemies
And from the hand of all who hate us,
To perform the mercy promised to our fathers
And to remember His holy covenant,
The promise which He swore to our father Abraham:
To grant us that we,
Being delivered from the hand of our enemies,
Might serve Him without fear,

In holiness and righteousness before Him all the days of our life.
And you, child, will be called the prophet of the Highest;
For you will go before the face of the Lord to prepare His ways,
To give knowledge of salvation to His people
By the remission of their sins,
Through the tender mercy of our God,
With which the Dayspring from on high has visited us;
To give light to those who sit in darkness and the shadow of death,
To guide our feet into the way of peace."

Mary left the presence of her Godly relatives and returned home to Nazareth, just after the 'Feast of Weeks'. As she made the journey home, she thought about Joseph. He would be wondering about the absence of his betrothed wife; she knew the time would come when she would need to share the news the Angel had brought, but when?

With the passing of some weeks, Mary realised she was pregnant. She knew the time had arrived to tell her betrothed Joseph everything that had happened to her. But how would he react? What could she expect?

With a quiet prayer to the Lord asking for His guidance, she visited Joseph.

"Good morning my love. What brings you to see me? Are you inquisitive about the progress of our room?" said Joseph.

In a voice that was apprehensive, filled with hesitancy, Mary said, "Joseph, I am sorry for being away so long. I have imagined your concern for me." She continued as Joseph focused his full attention on her. "You would remember some time ago, I was troubled and distant. It was nothing you did or said, but I had a visit by the angel Gabriel. He told me about my future, and after sharing with my parents, they thought it best for me to spend some time with my Uncle and Aunt," said Mary.

"But what was so important that you couldn't have confided in me? After all, we are betrothed," was Joseph's reply.

"Joseph, I am pregnant with God's Son!" said Mary.

There was no answer for some time, and then Joseph quietly said, "This is a lot to take in Mary. I need to think and pray about what you have told me," and with that, Joseph walked away, leaving Mary full of uncertainties.

Mary returned to her parent's home, to wait for Joseph's response. There was nothing more anyone could do. It was Joseph's decision and their lives were in his hands.

Although Joseph was a mature, just, God-fearing man, his first reaction was to think Mary had committed adultery. The penalty for adultery was public humiliation and being stoned to death. He could however, because of his love for his betrothed, choose to divorce her quietly. By doing this, he would share some of the blame and Mary would be able to live and have the child. But this was not God's plan.

Joseph was torn between his love for Mary and the requirement of the law. He prayed for the Lord's guidance and finally settled down to sleep. During the night, he had a dream.

"Joseph! Joseph, son of David! Listen to me," said an angel. The angel continued, *"Do not be afraid to take to you Mary your wife, for that which is conceived in her is of the Holy Spirit. She will bring forth a Son, and you shall call His name Jesus, for He will save His people from their sin. All this was done that it might be fulfilled which was spoken by the Lord through the prophet, saying: 'The virgin shall be with child and bear a Son, and they shall call His name Immanuel'."*

When Joseph awoke he realised he had been dreaming. He now understood the situation completely including his betrothed wife's involvement. Joseph trusted the Lord and accepted what was expected of him. He would marry Mary, and care for her and the child. They would marry when his father had approved the room he was building for them all.

Mary continued to make the necessary preparations for the birth of God's Son and the marriage to her betrothed Joseph. While her everyday tasks were a little different, she looked forward to when Joseph would come for her, and they could be a family unit.

But other events were about to change their plans. The Roman Emperor, Caesar Augustus, decreed that everyone in the Empire should be registered. Every man was required to go to his own city of birth. The Roman rulers wanted to be sure that subjects were paying sufficient taxes.

Joseph was busy in his carpenter's shop, when his father opened the door.

"Good morning, father. What has bought you into my shop? You look worried. What has happened? Is mother well?" asked Joseph.

"My son. The Governor has implemented a decree from the Emperor Caesar Augustus for a new tax system. We are required to register in Bethlehem, as that is our ancestral home. I have already talked with Mary's parents as they need to register as you do. We are not sure how our going will affect you and Mary," said Jacob, Joseph's father.

"Thank you, father, for your concern. All my life, you have been there for me. I will talk with Mary to decide what we will do. God will look after us all, even though this is not a good time for Mary, as it is not long until the Baby is to be born." And with those words, Jacob left the carpenter's shop while Joseph contemplated his best plan of action.

Joseph closed the shop when his days' work was done, and still contemplating their situation, made his way to Mary's home, where she was living with her parents.

"Greetings my beloved Mary. Are you keeping well?" said Joseph.

"Yes, very well, thank you." Mary indicated for him to enter the home.

"Please come inside. Our parents were just discussing the news of the forthcoming census. Maybe you can bring a solution to our plight," replied Mary.

Joseph entered the family room where the members of both families were sitting together.

"Son. Have you any thoughts?" asked Jacob.

Joseph hesitated, then with wise words replied, "I think we should all travel together to Bethlehem, if that is agreeable with you all. It's not the decree I am concerned with, but protecting Mary's well-being in this delicate time. What are your thoughts?"

Everyone was quiet for a few moments as they tried to consider what Joseph had said. Heli looked at his wife and then broke the silence. "I think that is a wonderful idea. What do the rest of you think?"

"I am in agreeance with you," said Jacob. "We should make plans to leave sufficient time for the journey. Mary would also have the care of our wives, Joseph."

"I believed our God would provide a solution for us all, as I knew He could. Praise be to God!" Joseph replied.

The days quickly passed, and with adequate preparation, the two families set out on the long journey to Bethlehem.

Joseph led the donkey, carefully selecting a smooth path for the donkey's feet, providing a comfortable ride for Mary. They were grateful for travelling in the spring season, as the temperatures during the daytime could be hot, but not as hot as the summer days.

Days passed and the group of travellers approached Jerusalem. Zacharias and Elizabeth's home would be a great place to relax and unwind before they continued their journey to Bethlehem. Mary and her parents would be able to see John, who was born almost one year before to Zacharias and Elizabeth. Mary remembered her Uncle Zacharias was visited by the same angel Gabriel. Gabriel told Zacharias, that his wife Elizabeth, who was known as barren, would have a child. What a joyous occasion for them all, especially as Zacharias could now speak and hear again.

Elizabeth was delighted to see her relatives and welcomed them with open arms.

"My dear sister and my beautiful blessed niece. Indeed! Welcome to you all. Come on in and make yourself comfortable in our guest rooms," said Elizabeth. The weary travellers were relieved the longest part of their journey was over.

After the travellers had settled in, Zacharias and Elizabeth introduced their son John to everyone. John was born when his parents were thought to be old, although his father was still performing his priestly duties in the temple. The young boy walked over to where Mary was sitting, looked at her and smiled. There appeared to be a bond between John, Mary and the unborn babe, formed when John was in his mother's womb.

When the two families were about to complete the last part of their journey to Bethlehem, Elizabeth suggested Joseph and Mary should stay for a little extra time, as Elizabeth had much to talk about with her niece. This was agreed upon, and Mary and Joseph bid their parents goodbye.

When the time was appropriate, Elizabeth came to Mary and Joseph. She presented them with a small package.

"My most blessed Mary and Joseph. I believe you should take these with you, for the birth of your baby. It is only right that God's Son should be protected when He is born. Use these swaddling cloths to wrap Him in," said Elizabeth as she addressed herself to them both. Joseph and Mary were thankful for her kindness, as many of the provisions for the baby's birth had been left back in Mary's parent's home in Nazareth.

Joseph and Mary farewelled Zacharias and Elizabeth and completed the short journey to Bethlehem, arriving on the 'Day of Preparation' for 'Passover'.

During the early part of the morning, the parents and children would play a symbolic game. The house would be cleaned from top to bottom. Every part of the house needed to be spotlessly cleaned, including the removal of any leaven. When this was completed, the father would hide a couple of pieces of leaven that the children would be encouraged to find. Once found, the children would call their parents, as they knew not to touch the leaven. The father would sweep each piece onto a wooden spoon with a feather, wrap it in a linen cloth and burn the parcel. The home was now ready for the feast of 'Passover', which the family would celebrate that evening after sundown.

It was customary for families to accommodate travelling relatives so Mary and Joseph made their way to the ancestral home. Many of the townsfolk greeted Joseph and Mary as they passed by. But when they arrived, they were stunned to find many additional family members already there. They had not anticipated so many extra relatives.

The host was troubled by the need to house everyone who had arrived for the census. The guest room was already full of relatives. The only room unoccupied was the stable area. The family's domestic animals would normally occupy a small part inside the home, but because it was springtime, the animals were outside.

Joseph and Mary were appreciative of the offer to stay in the stable, as the area was more than adequate for their needs. They could see the home, including the stable area, was spotlessly clean. God had provided the perfect place where His Son was to be born. A spotless place, for the spotless Son of God.

The time came for Mary to give birth to her precious Son. The female relatives helped and supported Mary, along with the local midwife, while the men congregated together, each father reassured Joseph his wife would be fine. When the Baby was born, He was wrapped in swaddling cloths.

Mary held Him close to herself while the other mothers and fathers, especially Joseph, admired the newly-born. The one Joseph loved dearly, had given birth to the Saviour of the world. God, through the Holy Spirit, was also present, as the promise to protect Mary was realised.

As the excitement of the birth of the baby subsided, Mary was prompted to lay her precious One, wrapped in swaddling cloths, in a manager that was normally used to feed the animals during the night. She knew He would be safe, and away from the traffic of the family. Unbeknown to Mary, Father God was also celebrating the birth of His Son.

Meanwhile, in a nearby field, a number of trainee priests were watching the unblemished lambs and sheep, which would be used in the temple sacrifices.

These trainees were Aaron, Enoch, Hiram, Hosea, Ira, Jordan, Levi, Nathan, Noah, Rueben, Seth and Solomon. It was a beautiful clear night and two of the young shepherds were talking to pass the time during the long hours of the night.

'Not much happening tonight, Ira,' said Enoch.

'Not quite so, my brother. I have noticed a glow in the night sky that is very unusual,' replied Ira.

Having heard the conversation, Jordan, Levi and Nathan joined them. All of a sudden, out of nowhere, an angel of the Lord stood before them. A light shone from the heavenly being, and the glory of the Lord encompassed them all. The young shepherds were so afraid; they huddled together in a bunch on the ground.

It was then the angel spoke to them, *"Do not be afraid, for behold, I bring you good tidings of great joy which will be for all people. For there is born to you this day in the city of David a Saviour, who is Christ the Lord. And this will be the sign to you. You will find a Babe wrapped in swaddling clothes, lying in a manger."*

The young men were awe-struck, lifting their heads cautiously to see what was happening. Then a great choir, a multitude of the heavenly hosts joined the angel and filled the night sky. They were praising God and singing,

"Glory to God in the highest,
and on earth peace,
goodwill toward men!"

And then the angelic beings were gone. Everything became quiet. Not even the sheep had stirred.

"I don't know about the rest of you, but I have never experienced anything like that before in my life," said Seth.

"Everything is so peaceful and quiet now. Did you notice the sheep and lambs did not move? They were not at all scared," said Solomon.

"I would like to go and see this Baby that the angel told us about. Anyone else interested?" said Nathan.

"Well, we can't all go. How about Jordan and I watch the sheep and lambs? They are content just sitting in their sheepfolds, and the rest of you go," said Levi.

And so, it was agreed. Away the young shepherds went, talking amongst themselves about all they had seen, heard and happened, as they hurried to Bethlehem.

It wasn't a long journey from the grazing areas and the sheepfolds to Bethlehem. As they moved quickly along the road and through the narrow streets, suddenly Ira said, "Look! There's a light and some noise coming from that house. Let's try there." Sure enough, they found a newly-born Baby wrapped in swaddling cloths, lying in a manger, with

His parents, Mary and Joseph next to Him, just as the angel had said.

Mary and Joseph, and the other family members were stunned that the shepherds would come to their home during the night. The young shepherds, full of excitement were eager to tell what had happened to them, what the angel had said, and how the heavenly hosts sang. The family members were totally amazed to hear this had taken place only a little distance from their family home, as they had not seen or heard a thing.

Mary's response was different. She sat quietly, taking in everything she heard. She would long remember the events of this evening.

So much had happened that night; the family members struggled to come to terms with all they had been told.

The shepherds on the other hand, were praising God as they bid the family farewell and made their way back to their sheep and lambs and the other shepherds. As they left, the shepherds told all the villagers about what they had seen and experienced during the night.

Within a few days, the household settled back into normal life. Most of the relatives had registered for the census so they left and returned to their homes. Joseph and Mary delayed their departure. Mary, having a baby, was required to complete a time of purification. According to Levitical Law, she was unclean for forty days, during which time she was confined to the home. Once the relatives had left, Joseph and Mary would have been given the guest room for themselves and the Baby.

During Mary's time of purification, according to custom, eight days after the birth, the baby was circumcised. It was also time for the newly-born babe to be named, and as Joseph was instructed, he named the baby Jesus.

At last, the time came for Joseph and Mary to return home to Nazareth. Jerusalem was only a short distance from Bethlehem, and Joseph and Mary could stay with Zacharias and Elizabeth, as the city was on the route home. It would also be an opportune time for Joseph and Mary to show the newly-born babe, Jesus to their hosts. Joseph and Mary bid farewell to their relatives in Bethlehem, and all the memories contained within the visit there, and made their way to Jerusalem.

When Joseph, Mary and Jesus arrived at Zacharias and Elizabeth's home, Elizabeth rushed to meet them, calling her husband excitedly. "Zacharias, John, come quickly! Look. Joseph and Mary have arrived, and Mary has her baby, cradled in her arms."

Elizabeth, filled with excitement, opened the door of their home. "Come in my blessed niece with your Holy Child."

"Joseph. Welcome to our home on this wonderful occasion," said Zacharias. John was quiet, as he gazed on the Babe Mary was holding.

"Come on in, all of you," said Elizabeth. "You must tell us all about your adventure. Your parents relayed some of what happened, but I am sure you have much detail to share with us. Oh Mary, Joseph, you are so blessed."

Joseph and Mary made their way to the guest room, where after Elizabeth had cradled Jesus in her arms, Mary placed Him in a crib. John had also used the crib previously.

"My dear Aunt Elizabeth. You are such a blessing to us," said Mary. "You knew we would need these swaddling cloths. Here they are returned to you. I can't ever thank you enough."

John stood at the crib, as he gazed on the One who lay there in his place.

Joseph and Zacharias had made their way to the living area and sat talking.

"Joseph, you are aware that the 'Feast of Weeks' is only a few days away. I do hope you will stay and attend with us, as I know your custom is to participate in these must-attend feasts in Jerusalem," said Zacharias.

"I would be most grateful to share your hospitality during this time. Mary and I also need to present Jesus at the temple and offer a sacrifice," said Joseph.

"Elizabeth and I would be honoured to assist in any way we can," replied Zacharias.

"Zacharias, it has been financially burdening for us over these past months although God has provided for us in ways we would never have imagined. Would you help me to secure two turtle doves for the prescribed sacrifice as I am unable to afford a lamb?" asked Joseph.

"Joseph, let the purchase of the two turtle doves be the least of your concerns. I count it a privilege to assist you in finding the right person so you can buy your offering," replied Zacharias.

After a few days, the time of Jesus' presentation at the temple arrived. It was only a short walk to the temple from Zacharias' home. Joseph, Mary, and Jesus, along with the two turtle doves, made their way through the busy Jerusalem streets and into the temple. Joseph was very familiar with the temple, as for many years, he had attended the feasts at least three times a year. Joseph and his family were directed to the place for the sacrifice was to be presented.

A priest named Simeon, much the same age as Zacharias, encouraged the family to come to him. Earlier that day, Simeon had been prompted to attend the temple. Simeon was one of a number of believers who were looking for the 'Consolation of Israel'. When Simeon gazed upon the Child he was holding in his arms, he exclaimed,

"Lord, now You are letting Your servant depart in peace, according to Your word; for my eyes have seen Your salvation which You have prepared before the face of all peoples, a light to bring revelation to the Gentiles, and the glory of Your people Israel."

Joseph and Mary both marvelled at what Simeon had said about their Child. After Simeon had blessed them both, he directed his next remarks directly to Mary.

"This Child is destined for the fall and rising of many in Israel, and for a sign which will be spoken against yes, a sword will pierce through your own soul also, that the thoughts of many hearts may be revealed."

As Jesus' presentation was complete, Joseph, Mary and Jesus began to make their way out of the temple.

As they were about to leave, a prophetess by the name of Anna, gazed upon the baby Jesus and instantly gave thanks to the Lord for this One. She told all those who believed in the redemption of Israel, she had seen the Redeemer.

When Joseph and Mary, holding the Babe, Jesus, left the temple, they were in awe with everything that happened during the presentation.

Mary cradled Jesus in her arms and Joseph guided her steps as they descended the Temple Mount.

"Well, my betrothed, what did you make of all we have seen and heard today, regarding you and our Child," said Joseph.

"Joseph, I am not at all sure about what has happened since we left our homes in Nazareth. I could have never imagined what we have experienced over the past weeks could have ever happened, and especially to me. What made me so special, favoured, that our God would choose me for His plan to be carried out? I have no idea what His plan for the future holds for us either. I am blessed to have you. You have shown me so much love in the way you care for me. In this, I am truly blessed," replied Mary.

"My love, I too do not know what our God has in store for us. I know, we will be told all in His time. We just need to trust Him in all our ways," replied Joseph.

When they had completed all things according to the Law of the Lord, they returned to Galilee, to their own city, Nazareth.

When they arrived at Nazareth, Mary went to her parent's home and eagerly waited for Joseph to return and claim her as his bride. Joseph's return to collect his bride was dependent on his father's approval of the new room, for his new bride. Only then, could the two be married. Joseph never knew his wife, until the marriage was performed.

The family unit settled into what would seem normal family life. Joseph continued in his carpenter's shop, Mary looked after Jesus and the room prepared for them all. While life went on, unexpected events can cause havoc. Other things were taking place that Joseph, Mary and Jesus had no knowledge about.

Away in the east, some Wise Men had seen a star that indicated a king was born. The newly-born king was no ordinary king, as He was born, 'King of the Jews'.

Issachar sat at the very large table as he did most nights, mapping the night sky. Nothing much changed as he made some notes on the chart before him. Jotham was also mapping the section assigned to him when he suddenly noticed Issachar grabbing other charts and looking at them. He seemed puzzled and perplexed.

Jotham left his place and walked over to Issachar. Charts were everywhere. Issachar, of all people, was never disorganised. He was methodical and ordered. Jotham broke the silence and said, "Issachar! What are you doing? Why are your charts all over the place and not in order?"

"Jotham! Look to the night sky in the area I am plotting. What do you notice?" exclaimed Issachar.

Jotham took one of the charts and peered into the night sky. He looked once, then looked again. Jotham picked up another chart and looked a third time.

"Do you see it? There is a new star and it has only just appeared. The new star is not an ordinary star. This one is special," said Issachar.

"You are right Issachar. We must confer with the others. Make sure you mark the exact location," said Jotham as he left to wake some of the other astronomers.

Very shortly, Jotham returned with some astronomers following him. Othniel was the first to speak.

"What's all this about a new star, Issachar?" said Othniel, the head astronomer. "This better be worth waking me from my sleep. Now, what do you think you have found?"

More astronomers had also joined the group. There were Kemuel, Matthias, Zebadiah, Tobias, and Lemuel, all peering at the chart in front of Issachar.

"I was just completing my usual work, when I noticed something was not right," said Issachar.

"All right, all right, get on with it. What did you see?" snapped Othniel.

"Look, here at the chart." Issachar pointed to a newly marked position. All eyes watched his hands as they moved.

"Now, look into the heavens. Tell me what you see?" Issachar said with an overwhelming sense of joy in his voice. Everyone, without exception, looked into the clear night sky. Sighs were heard as each one contemplated what this new star meant.

"Well done Issachar. You are very observant. Make sure you note all the facts in your report," replied Othniel. He continued, "My fellow astronomers, we need to meet very early in the morning. This is no ordinary star. Please get plenty of sleep as we need to discuss what the appearance of this significant star means for us all." Othniel looked again at Issachar, who was beaming with joy, and said, "Well done Issachar."

The response of the astronomers was unanimous. The star was very special, as the appearance signified the birth of a king, but not just any king. The star indicated that the 'King of the Jews' had been born.

After much talk, the decision was made to worship the One born 'King of the Jews'. These Hebrew astronomers were a remnant of those taken into exile, many years previously. They, like Simeon, Anna and others were waiting for the Redeemer of Israel. Their long-awaited Messiah had been born. Gifts were chosen, which would be fitting for a King, not only a King but the Redeemer of mankind.

Adonijah, although not an astronomer, was responsible for the entourage that would travel to Jerusalem, after all, this was a Jewish city and the palace was there. Where else would such an important King reside. Adonijah thought it best to follow the normal trade route from their home in the east to Jerusalem. This road would provide considerable protection from bands of robbers who often attacked lone travellers.

The journey took many days, but eventually, the mixed group of astronomers, carers, cooks and servants, finally came to the palace in Jerusalem. What a relief to be at their destination. It would only be a short time before they could make the long trek home, back to their own country.

As the astronomers or Wise Men made their way to the palace gate, they were stopped by the guards.

"Halt! Who goes there?" was the stern command.

"Sir, we are Astronomers, err, Wise Men from the east. We have travelled many miles to worship the One born 'King of the Jews'. Would you be kind enough to arrange an audience with the King for us please?" said Othniel.

"Wait here! I will make some inquiries for you," said a rather intimidating Roman guard. When the guard returned, he told the travellers to follow him.

"Come along my fellow astronomers. Not long now," was the cheerful reply from Othniel.

To their dismay, the guard led them to Herod, the reigning king.

"What is it you require? The guard babbled on about you wanting an audience with a King of the Jews. There is no such King here. What are you on about?" barked Herod.

"Your majesty. With all due respect, we Wise Men from the east saw His star in the night sky some sixteen months ago. The appearance of the star signified that the 'King of the Jews' had been born. We have spent much time as we travelled a long way with the express intent to worship Him. We ask that you merely direct us to where He is, and we would conduct our business with Him and be gone," said Othniel.

When Herod had processed all the Wise Men had said, he became troubled and perplexed within himself. Herod thought, *who was the One born to be King? This is a rival to me. I need to eradicate Him.*

"Gentlemen, astronomers, whoever you are," Herod said sarcastically. "Kindly sit over there. Make yourselves comfortable and I will make some inquiries on your behalf," said Herod as he left his throne room.

Herod made his way straight to the High priest and his scribes.

"Priest! What do you know about a King of the Jews?" demanded Herod.

"Your majesty. I have heard nothing about the birth of a king, and especially One who is born 'King of the Jews'," said the high priest.

"Well, I have a party of Wise Men from the eastern part of the world, sitting in my throne room. They saw a star which indicated a 'King of the Jews' was born, and they expected Him to be here! I want some answers, and I want them now! Do you hear me!" roared Herod.

The high priest knew very well not to infuriate the King, so he called all the priests and scribes together. Maybe they could fabricate something that would appease the king. To the chief priest's surprise, some knew exactly what was happening. When they were asked where the Christ was to be born, the reply came, *"In Bethlehem of Judah."* They also backed up their answer with scripture written by the prophet Micah. *"But you, Bethlehem, in the land of Judah, are not the least among the rulers of Judah; for out of you shall come a Ruler Who will shepherd My people Israel."* Herod was pleased with the information from the scribes and priests.

Herod hurried back to the Wise Men, as a cunning plan formed in his mind. "Gentlemen, I have good news for you. The One you are seeking is in Bethlehem. It is only a short distance from Jerusalem. Let me encourage you all to seek diligently in this rather small town of my region, and when you find your King, please return and tell me where He is so I can also go and worship Him," said Herod pleasantly.

The astronomers thanked the king for this new information and made their way out of his presence.

When Othniel told Adonijah about the meeting with Herod, he assembled the entourage in readiness for the small distance to Bethlehem. Issachar and Jotham, were somewhat upset as were the other astronomers, as their journey was not yet complete. Suddenly, without warning, the star they had seen previously, sixteen months earlier, reappeared. Issachar said, "Look! Look! The star has reappeared."

Despair was replaced with joy. Othniel just smiled at Issachar. At the reappearance of the star, this entourage of people followed the path of the star, but to their surprise, the star headed in a northerly direction, not south. Where was the elusive star leading them?

Day after day, the travellers followed the star, increasingly surprised at the direction it was taking.

"Othniel," said Adonijah. "Didn't you say Bethlehem was our destination?"

"Adonijah, you like us, believe in the Messiah. The star reappearing was no coincidence. We believe the star is God's messenger and will take us to the King," Othniel replied reassuringly. And so, they continued to follow the star all the way to Nazareth, where it stood over a home.

"Adonijah, Issachar, Jotham. Our journey is at an end in this most unlikely place," said Othniel. He made his way to the door of the little home and knocked. A lady opened the door. As she looked out over a multitude of people outside her home, she said, "How can I help you, sir?"

"We are looking for the 'King for the Jews'. Can you help us?" said Othniel.

A man had joined the lady. He looked a little bemused at the crowd before him. "I believe we can. I am Mary and this is my husband Joseph. Those of you who can, please accompany us inside," said Mary as she took the hand of her husband for some support.

Joseph, Mary and Jesus, who was holding the hands of His parents, stood before the crowd gathered in their home. Joseph spoke with the voice of a clarion, "This is Jesus, God's Son, born the Son of David, the King of the Jews."

As those words were spoken, the whole assembly knelt before Jesus and worshipped Him. Words like, "Praise be to God for evidence of our Redeemer! Behold our Messiah! Blessed be the Name of the Lord!" could be heard over and over, resounding around and around the room.

When the worship had subsided, gifts were placed at the feet of the young child, Jesus. The first was 'Gold'. The gift for a king. The second was 'Frankincense'. A gift for a priest. The third was 'Myrrh'. The gift for one who is to die. As their task was completed, the Wise Men bid farewell to the household.

The wise travellers set up a camp in the fields nearby. Othniel looked at Issachar who was stargazing and said, "Issachar, I could never have imagined, what you discovered on that night so long ago, would have taken us on the journey we have experienced. I will be ever indebted to you for all you have done, not only for me, but for us all. Thank you, my colleague, no, my friend."

Issachar had no idea how to respond to Othniel, for the journey had changed all their lives, and for the better. He just smiled and soon, all were asleep.

The next morning, Adonijah was eager to get the entourage heading back to Jerusalem and to the palace, where he knew Herod would be waiting. But this was not to be.

Jotham approached Issachar and said, "I had the weirdest dream last night."

"I had a weird dream too," said Issachar. "What did you dream, Jotham?"

"An angel warned me not to go back to Jerusalem and Herod," replied Jotham.

"I had the same dream," said Issachar. "What do you think it means, Jotham?"

Before either could reply, Othniel spoke up. "Well, you aren't the only ones to have dreams. I had the same dream as both of you. I believe we have been warned by God not to return to our home through Jerusalem."

When Adonijah heard what was said, he informed the entourage, they would make their homeward journey without passing through Jerusalem.

Joseph had returned to his carpentry, and Mary cared for Jesus and their home. Their days passed happily until Joseph had a dream. He gently touched Mary to wake her.

"Joseph, Joseph, it's still dark. Why have you woken me?" said Mary.

"Mary. We need to leave. We need to leave straight away," said Joseph in an alarming voice.

"Why Joseph? What has happened?" replied Mary.

"The Lord warned me in a dream to take you and Jesus and flee to Egypt. Egypt, of all places. I have no idea why, but we need to be obedient. You wake Jesus. I'll get the donkeys," said Joseph.

Mary hurriedly gathered a few necessities, quietly asking God for guidance as she packed. "Wake up my precious Jesus. Daddy has been warned in a dream about something bad that will happen, and we need to leave our home straightaway. Get some of Your special things and put them in a bag. Bless You Jesus," said Mary.

As they left their home, they wondered why God had directed them to flee. They quickly called at both of the parent's homes and briefly shared with them what the angel had revealed to Joseph. When they would return was totally unknown. As Joseph planned the way to Egypt, Samaria was not an option. The family needed to pass through the very heart of Jerusalem, where Herod and the palace were situated. Joseph and Mary were confident in Father God, who had promised to overshadow them all. They knew God would be true to His promise, and so they left, not knowing when or if they would return.

Meanwhile, back in the palace, Herod was waiting for the return of the wise men. He was curious about what they found. Day after day turned into week after week, and still no sign of the astronomers. Herod became increasingly anxious. He wanted news of the new King who threatened his reign.

"Where are those wise men, I want that boy killed," shouted Herod in a rage.

"Scribe! Scribe! Come here immediately," screamed Herod.

"Yes, your majesty. How can I serve you?" inquired the scribe, bowing in Herod's presence.

"Fetch me all the Census records from the Bethlehem area," commanded Herod.

"Certainly, your worship. I will return shortly with the scrolls as they have been stored away," replied the scribe.

"Listen! I want them now and I want them here. Do you understand me scribe?"

"I will make haste," your majesty.

As soon as the scribe returned, Herod meticulously went through every person, as the scribe noted any Herod thought to be important or of interest. He was determined to find this one born to be 'King of the Jews' and dispose of Him once and for all.

When Herod was satisfied with what he had found, he dismissed the scribe and summoned the guard.

"Captain of the guard!" shouted Herod.

"I am here at your command. What do you require?" came the reply.

"Go to Bethlehem and all its districts. Travel as far as you need. Your area may well extend to Nazareth. Kill all the male children two years and under of all the parents who were at Bethlehem for the census. Yes, two years old and under," shouted Herod.

"Your wish is my command, Sire," said the guard.

As the guard left, one could hear Herod mutter under his breath, "Disobey me will you? I'll have my way, you can count on that."

All the boys and male babies that had been in Bethlehem and throughout the region, two years of age and under were put to death. Herod's actions fulfilled the prophecy of Jeremiah the prophet when he wrote:

"A voice was heard in Ramah, lamentations, weeping, and great mourning, Rachel weeping for her children, refusing to be comforted, because they are no more."

With the passing of a few years, Herod died. An angel of the Lord appeared to Joseph in a dream.

"Joseph. Joseph. I am an angel, and I have a message from the Lord. *Arise, take your young Child and His mother, and go to the land of Israel, for those who sought the young Child's life are dead."*

When Joseph woke up, he noticed Mary was also awake. He looked at her and smiled, then said, "Mary, I have some good news. We are going home. An angel told me it is safe to do so. Isn't that great!" said Joseph.

"Oh Joseph, that is great news. How good it will be to see our parents again. Jesus, Jesus. We are going home," said Mary.

And they dwelt in a city called Nazareth, that it might be fulfilled which was spoken by the prophets, "He shall be called a Nazarene."

The Shepherds. Hebrew name and meaning.
Aaron: "Exalted one."
Enoch: "Dedicated."
Hiram:" Exalted brother."
Hosea: "Salvation."
Ira: "Watchful."
Jordan: "To flow down" or "descend."
Levi: "Joining" or "adhering."
Nathan: "Gift."
Noah: "Rest" or "comfort."
Reuben: "Behold, a son."
Seth: "Appointed."
Solomon: "Peaceful."

The Wise Men. Hebrew name and meaning.
Othniel: "Lion of God; the hour of God."
Issachar: "Reward; recompense."
Jotham: "The perfection of the Lord."
Kemuel: "God hath raised up."
Matthias: "The gift of the Lord."
Zebadiah: "Portion of the Lord; the Lord is my portion."
Tobias: "The Lord is good."
Lemuel: "God with them."
Adonijah: "The Lord is my master."

Part Two

Hidden Lessons in The Christmas Story

Introduction

Many of the significant events in Jesus' life occurred during the Feasts of Israel. The Seven Feasts foreshadowed Christ's first coming, His crucifixion, His resurrection and His second coming. The Feasts will be mentioned throughout the text, and clarified for your understanding, in line with the appropriate event in Christ's nativity and childhood.

Most people have some understanding of the sequence of events of the Nativity, however the Biblical accounts have led many people to believe the events happened in a matter of a few months. Digging deeper into the account, the accepted version of Christ's birth, will be compared to the in-depth record as told in the Bible about the birth of Jesus. As Christmas is all about the Birth of Jesus Christ, all associated events are included for your knowledge and understanding. Many hidden lessons are contained within the account of the Christ Child.

Four verses of scripture seem to underline the whole narrative of the 'Birth of Christ'.

The first was all about the mission of Jesus Christ. *"For the Son of Man has come to seek and to save the lost"* (Luke 19:10).

The second scripture says, *"He came to His own, and His own did not receive Him"* (John 1:11).

The third and fourth verses give hope for those who seek the Messiah as their Redeemer. *"But as many as received Him, to them He gave the right to become children of God, to those who believe on His name: who were born, not of blood, nor of the will of the flesh, nor of the will of man, but of God"* (John 1:12-13).

To help understand the events of Christ's nativity, and the sequence of events, as recorded in the Gospels, we need to understand what the 'Feasts of Israel' are and the significance of each for the Jewish people.

In the first part, the Feasts of Israel and their significance for the Jewish people is covered, followed by how each Feast is related to Christ's birth.

The second part will establish the links between the sequence of the Feasts and Christ's birth.

The third part retells *'The Christmas Story'*, as generally accepted today.

The fourth part, *'Hidden Lessons in the Christmas Story'*, outlines my reasons for challenging many of the traditional interpretations of the events associated with Christ's birth. I have studied the original texts and researched cultural behaviours in biblical times to support my views.

The conclusion is a short story the author has written called, *'From the Cradle to the Grave'.* This is an allegory about a small portion of the life of Jesus Christ.

The Feasts of Israel, and the Life of Jesus the Christ

I have or some time believed Jesus was born and died on Passover. Passover and the Day of Preparation for the Sabbath were the same day that year. While no actual proof is available to substantiate this claim, by looking at the events associated with the order of the Feasts of Israel, I have found sufficient evidence to support my theory. Let's explore each festival and compare the festivals with the events in Jesus' birth and childhood.

The year of our Saviour's birth, Jesus Christ is obscured because there is no conclusive date for Herod's death. Rather than try to prove a year, I will look at the seasons. While historians may choose different years for an event, seasons each year, remain stable. I have accepted Christ's birth as Passover. Passover was usually in late March to early April and is the season of Spring in the Holy Land.

So, what are the Feasts of Israel and what are the significant events in the birth of Jesus? Let's make two lists comparing the Feasts of Israel with the known events.

1. The Passover.	The Birth of Jesus.
2. Feast of Unleavened Bread.	Joseph attended the celebration at the temple in Jerusalem.
3. Feast of Firstfruits.	Joseph and the family continue to celebrate.
4. Feast of Weeks.	Jesus presented at the Temple in Jerusalem.
5. Feast of Trumpets.	The Wise Men worship the child Jesus.
6. Yon Kippur.	The Flight into Egypt.
7. Feast of Tabernacles.	Living in Egypt.

Let us now take each 'Feast', discover what it means and then compare the findings to the associated event.

1 The Passover

Nisan 14. March/April Spring Feast. Lev. 23:5, Matt. 26:2.

Passover celebrates redemption; Christ the Passover

Lamb was slain at Calvary for the sins of the world.

The Passover lamb was the animal God directed the Israelites to use as a sacrifice in Egypt on the night God struck down the firstborn sons of every household (Exod. 12:29). This was the final plague God issued against Pharaoh, and it led to Pharaoh releasing the Israelites from slavery (Exod. 11:1). After that fateful night, God instructed the Israelites to observe the Passover Feast as a lasting memorial (Exod. 12:14). God instructed every household of the Israelite people to select a year-old male lamb without defect (Exod. 12:5, Lev. 22:20-21). The head of the household was to slaughter the lamb at twilight, taking care that none of its bones were broken, and apply some of its blood to the tops and sides of the doorframe of the house. The lamb was to be roasted and eaten (Exod. 12:7-8). God also gave specific instructions to the Israelites for their conduct during the meal, "with your cloak tucked into your belt, your sandals on your feet and your staff in your hand" (Exod. 12:11, Eph. 6:14). In other words, they had to be ready to travel. God said that when He saw the lamb's blood on the doorframe of a house, He would 'pass over' that home and not permit 'the destroyer' (Exod. 12:23) to enter. Any home without the blood of the lamb would have their firstborn son struck down that night (Exod. 12: 12-13).

The New Testament establishes a relationship between the Passover lamb and Jesus Christ (1Cor. 5:7). The prophet

John the Baptist recognized Jesus as *"the Lamb of God"* (John 1:29), and the apostle Peter links the lamb without defect (Exod. 12:5) with Christ, whom he calls a *"lamb without blemish or defect"* (1Peter 1:19). Jesus is qualified to be called One "without blemish" because His life was completely free from sin (Heb. 4:15). In Revelation, John the apostle saw Jesus as *"a Lamb, looking as if it had been slain"* (Rev. 5:6). The Bible says believers have symbolically applied the sacrificial blood of Christ to their hearts and thus have escaped eternal death (Heb. 9:12, 14). Just as the Passover lamb's applied blood caused the 'destroyer' to pass over each household, Christ's applied blood causes God's judgment to pass over sinners and gives life to believers (Rom. 6:23).

The first Passover marked the Hebrews' release from Egyptian slavery. The Passover Lamb in the Old Testament had a specific purpose however, it was a mere foreshadowing of the better and final Passover Lamb, Jesus Christ. Through His sinless life and sacrificial death, Jesus became the only One capable of providing people with a way to escape death and a sure hope of eternal life (1Peter 1:20-21). Jesus was born to die for our sins. He was the Sacrificial Lamb.

2 *Feast of Unleavened Bread*

Unleavened Bread. Nisan 15. March/April. Spring Feast. Lev. 23:6, Deut. 16:8.

Unleavened Bread represents sanctification. Jesus was

set apart. His body would not decay in the grave.

The Feast of Unleavened Bread was the first 'Must-attend Feast'. God set down specific feasts that were to be attended. *"Three times a year all your males shall appear before the Lord your God in the place which He chooses: at the Feast of Unleavened Bread, at the Feast of Weeks, and at the Feast of Tabernacles; and they shall not appear before the Lord empty-handed"* (Deut. 16:16).

Although not Jews, we who have accepted Jesus Christ as our Lord and Saviour, have attended the first must-attend feast. The word 'Sanctification' means, 'declaring something holy'. Leaven in the Bible represents sin. Unleavened means without leaven or the sin has been removed. Once we have accepted Jesus as our Saviour, we are cleansed or made holy by His shed blood, we are cleansed, and Jesus has become the substitute sacrificial Lamb, for our salvation.

Leaven caused fermentation. Paul, when writing to the Galatians says, *"A little leaven leavens the whole lump"* (Gal. 5:9). In other words, all sin needs to be removed. Because Jesus was God's Son, His body was resurrected before any decay would take place. Sin had no place in Him, as He was and will always be the spotless Son of God.

The day before 'Passover' was the day of preparation. The home would be thoroughly cleaned or cleansed of any leaven. Leaven represents sin. Children participated in a game to cleanse the home. After the home had been cleaned, a couple of pieces of leaven would be hidden and the children were encouraged to seek and find the leaven, as the father lit the way with a candle. When the leaven is found, the father warns the children not to touch it but uses a feather to sweep the leaven onto a wooden spoon that he then wraps in a linen cloth. This is then taken and burnt in the fire. Today we find a parallel when God removes the leaven from our lives. The Holy Spirit reveals areas of our lives where sin is to be found. The Holy Spirit then sweeps our sin onto the wooden cross of Jesus, wraps it in the linen burial cloth and eradicates the sin totally from our life. The fire of the Holy Spirit cleanses us from all sin.

The home where Jesus was born would have been cleansed of leaven. This was very important because the birthplace of our Lord had to be clean. When Joseph and Mary arrived at the home in Bethlehem, the guest room was full of relatives. They were offered a place, which during winter, was shared with the animals. As it was spring, the animals would have been outside for the duration of Mary and Joseph's stay and Jesus' birth. The whole house would have been cleansed of leaven. The spotless Lamb of God was born in a spotless place prepared for Him.

Joseph would have attended the Feast of Unleavened Bread in Jerusalem. Joseph would have many reasons to praise God for the safe deliverance of the Child and Mary.

3 *Feast of Firstfruits*

Nisan 16. March/April, May/June. Spring Feast. Lev. 23:10, Luke 24:7

The term Firstfruits means, 'there is more to come'. The Firstfruits were the first gathering of the barley harvest. When the priest waved the sheaves of the barley harvest before the Lord as the Firstfruits offering, he was thanking God for the abundant harvest that was about to follow.

Jesus, the Messiah, the Firstfruits of the Resurrection, meant He was the first of the resurrection that would never see death again. The abundance of the harvest of the resurrection means there will be an abundance of resurrected souls in the future.

The Feast of Firstfruits foreshadows the Lord's triumphant resurrection; death simply could not hold her foe. On the third day, Jesus rose victoriously from the grave.

Because Jesus Christ rose from the grave, we have the assurance of new life in Him. He conquered death! Paul when writing to the Corinthians says, *"So when corruptible must put on incorruption, and mortal has put on immortality, then shall be bought to pass the saying that is written: 'Death is swallowed up in victory'. O Death, where is your sting? O Hades, where is your victory? The sting of death is sin, and the strength of sin is the law. But thanks be to God, who gives us the victory through our Lord Jesus Christ"* (1Cor. 15:54-57).

The 'Feast of Firstfruits' foreshadows Jesus' resurrection, as He became the first fruit to be offered to Father God, as an acceptable sacrifice to redeem man from the curse of the law that was sin.

I would direct you to Revelation 12:1 to 6 for the birth of Jesus.

Now a great sign appeared in heaven: a woman clothed with the sun,
with the moon under her feet,
and on her head a garland of twelve stars.
2 Then being with child, she cried out in
labour and in pain to give birth.
3 And another sign appeared in heaven: behold, a great,
fiery red dragon having seven heads and ten horns,
and seven diadems on his heads.
4 His tail drew a third of the stars of heaven and
threw them to the earth.
And the dragon stood before the woman who was
ready to give birth,
to devour her Child as soon as it was born.
5 She bore a male Child who was to rule all nations
with a rod of iron.
And her Child was caught up to God and His throne.
6 Then the woman fled into the wilderness,
where she has a place prepared by God,
that they should feed her there one thousand two hundred
and sixty days.

To follow on, v7 to v12, because the Saviour of the world is born.

7 And war broke out in heaven: Michael and
his angels fought with the dragon;
and the dragon and his angels fought,
8 but they did not prevail,
nor was a place found for them in heaven any longer.
9 So the great dragon was cast out, that serpent of old,
called the Devil and Satan, who deceives the whole world;
he was cast to the earth, and his angels were cast out with him.
10 Then I heard a loud voice saying in heaven,
"Now salvation, and strength,
and the kingdom of our God, and the power of
His Christ have come,
for the accuser of our brethren, who accused them
before our God day and night,
has been cast down.
11 And they overcame him by the blood of the Lamb
and by the word of their testimony,
and they did not love their lives to the death.
12 Therefore rejoice, O heavens, and you who dwell in them!
Woe to the inhabitants of the earth and the sea!
For the devil has come down to you, having great wrath,
because he knows that he has a short time."

Satan is cast out of heaven, a defeated foe. Verses 13 to 17.

13 Now when the dragon saw that he had been cast to the earth,
he persecuted the woman who gave birth to the male Child.

14 But the woman was given two wings of a great eagle,
that she might fly into the wilderness to her place,
where she is nourished for a time and times and half a time,
from the presence of the serpent.
15 So the serpent spewed water out of his mouth like a flood after the woman,
that he might cause her to be carried away by the flood.
16 But the earth helped the woman,
and the earth opened its mouth and swallowed up the flood
which the dragon had spewed out of his mouth.
17 And the dragon was enraged with the woman,
and he went to make war with the rest of her offspring,
who keep the commandments of God and have the testimony of Jesus Christ.

Satan is now waging war with the Jews. Jesus, some 33 years in the future would fulfil this feast.

Paul when writing to the Corinthian Church says, *"But now is Christ risen from the dead and become the first fruits of them that slept"* (1Cor. 15:20). Paul had in mind the first sheaf (Firstfruits) of the barley harvest (Lev. 23:10). When God accepted the Firstfruits, they became the guarantee that the rest of the crop would indeed be harvested. Jesus, Himself is the 'Firstfruits' (1Cor. 15:23). Jesus was the first to be resurrected from death and the grave, never to die again. He alone is the 'Firstfruits'. Because Jesus was accepted, so are all those in Him. Because Jesus was resurrected, so will those who belong to Him.

4 *Feast of Weeks*

Sivan 6. 50 days after Passover. May/June. Spring Feast.
Exod. 34:33, Lev. 23:15-16, Deut. 16:10-16, 2Chron. 8:13.

The Feast of Weeks, also known as Shavuot, is an ancient grain harvest festival marking the beginning of the wheat harvest. It is also identified with the giving of the Torah on Mt. Sinai. Traditionally, the Book of Ruth is read, which conveys greenery and flowers. These are often used to decorate homes during Shavuot because Mount Sinai was thought to have burst into bloom in anticipation of God's word. The Feast of Weeks is fifty days from Passover.

Other events took place between Jesus' birth and His presentation in the Temple at Jerusalem. Jesus was circumcised eight days after being born (Luke 2:21). Mary's purification time was thirty-three days (Lev. 12:2-8) after the birth, she was not allowed to touch any hallowed thing. If the Wise Men had shown up in this time, she would not have been able to touch the gifts given to Jesus. After the birth, a mother was in isolation for forty days until she was now perceived as clean. Once the time was fulfilled, Mary was able to move out of the home and once more meet her friends. This also meant she could travel. Fifty days from 'Passover' is 'Feast of Weeks'.

It seemed reasonable that Joseph and Mary would want to attend the second must-attend feast in Jerusalem and present their baby at that time.

Joseph and Mary went to Jerusalem (Luke 2:22) to present Jesus at the Temple with the required sacrifices, at the Feast of Weeks. This would be the second 'Must-attend Feast' (Deut. 16:16). The Holy Spirit led Simeon to the Temple on this particular day (Luke 2:25 to 29). Simeon also prophesied over the child (Luke 2:29 to 32). Let me share with you the last verse of his Prophecy. *"A light to bring revelation to the Gentiles, and the glory of Your people Israel"* (Luke 2:32). The Prophecy refers to the coming of the Holy Spirit to the Gentiles. What better day for the prophecy to be spoken over Jesus than in the Temple at the feast time. Anna, a prophetess also gave witness of Jesus, to those who looked for the redemption in Jerusalem (Luke 2:36 to 38).

As Joseph and Mary had obeyed all the Levitical law required, I read the following. *"So, when they had performed all things according to the law of the Lord, they returned to Galilee, to their own city, Nazareth. And the Child grew and became strong in spirit, filled with wisdom; and the grace of God was upon Him"* (Luke 2:39 to 40). The family is no longer in Bethlehem but have returned to their home in Nazareth.

For Christians, The Feast of Weeks is celebrated as Pentecost, symbolizing God's gift of the Holy Spirit that inaugurated the New Covenant and Church Age. Forty days after Passover, Jesus ascended into heaven. Jesus told His followers not to depart from Jerusalem until the promise of the Father had been given to them (Acts 1:4). Ten days passed, *"And suddenly there came a sound from heaven, as of a rushing mighty wind, and it filled the whole house where they were sitting. Then there appeared to them divided tongues, as of fire, and one sat upon each of them. And they were all filled with the Holy Spirit and began to speak with other tongues, as the Spirit gave them utterance"* (Acts 2:3-4). While people previously bought the first fruits of their harvest, Father God was now offering the gift of the Holy Spirit, the first fruit being the resurrected Jesus Christ, to power the lives of those who had committed themselves to Jesus Christ.

5 *Feast of Trumpets*

Tishri 1-2 (new moon) September/October. Fall Feast.

The Feast of Trumpets is commanded in Leviticus 23:23-25. It is a Memorial Day announced with a blast of Trumpets and a day of solemn rest and includes a food offering to the Lord. It is a call to repentance in preparation for the Day of Atonement, which follows ten days later.

[23] Then the Lord spoke to Moses, saying,
[24] "Speak to the children of Israel, saying:
'In the seventh month, on the first day of the month,

you shall have a Sabbath-rest,
a memorial of blowing of trumpets,
a holy convocation.
[25] You shall do no customary work on it;
and you shall offer an offering made by fire to the Lord.'"

The day is not so much about celebrating, but rather meditating on one's life and giving glory to God. The latter is most definitely a reason to be joyous, but this holiday is also a reminder of the Creator's judgment over creation.

The shofar, which is more a horn than a trumpet, is a very important instrument in the history of Israel.

The Feast of Trumpets should coincide with the visit of the Wise Men. While they saw a star or sign in the east, nothing was guiding them, only their own calculations that took them to the Palace. Where else would you expect to find a king? We need to refer to Matthew's account to obtain a continuation of the events (Matt. 2:1 to 18). A brief account of this event tells us that the Wise Men arrived at the Palace in Jerusalem asking to see the new King. Herod had no such knowledge of the birth of a king asked the chief priests and scribes who told him that Bethlehem in Judea was the place where the Christ was to be born. Herod secretly asked when the Wise Men saw the star. Now having this information, he sent them to Bethlehem (Matt. 2:8a), telling them to search carefully for the young child, and then inform him, so he too could worship the King. The Wise Men left to continue their mission.

It is important to have as many of the facts as possible. Let me share two verses with you. *"When they heard the king, they departed; and behold, the star which they had seen in the East went before them, till it came and stood over where the young child was. When they saw the star, they rejoiced with exceeding great joy"* (Matt. 2:10 to 11). These Wise Men were travelling to Bethlehem in search of the Child, but something changed their minds. The star or sign they had seen in the East suddenly reappeared which bought them exceeding great joy. It didn't lead them to Bethlehem, but to a home in Nazareth, where it stood over where the young Child was. I am reminded that it was an angel of the Lord *stood* before the shepherds (Luke 2:8), was it also the angel of the Lord that *stood* over where the young child was? Did they need to wait until the night to see this sight or was this during the day? It is hard to see stars with your eyes in the daytime.

We are told they sought the child and worshipped Him (Matt. 2:11). There is another verse we need to consider. *"Then Herod, when he saw that he was deceived by the wise men, was exceedingly angry; and he sent forth and put to death all the male children who were in Bethlehem and in all its districts, from two years old and under, according to the time which he had determined from the wise men"* (Matt. 2:16). Most consider

Jesus to be around the age of sixteen months when the wise men arrived. It would have been well over a year following the birth of Jesus when the Wise Men arrived. We would then accept Jesus was about sixteen months old. Why is this important?

To answer the question, one would accept that a time has elapsed between the birth and the arrival of the Wise Men. Just as Mary was unaware of when Joseph would come for her, his bride, so we are unaware of when Jesus Christ will return to take His bride to be with Him. Just as the Wise Men came to the home in Nazareth unexpectedly, so too will Jesus Christ return be as *'A thief in the night'* (Matt. 24:44, 1Thess. 5:2, Rev.16:15).

The first four feasts followed concurrently, the fifth feast, the 'Feast of Trumpets', is celebrated in September. The Christians look with anticipation for the return of Christ, as we believe, at the sounding of the trumpet, Jesus will appear and claim His own, which is yet to happen in our time (Matt. 24:24:31, 1Cor. 15:52, 1Thess. 4:16). As we know Jesus Christ will return, we continue living every day looking for His return. Paul, when writing to the Philippians says, *"Therefore God also has highly exalted Him and given Him the name which is above every name, that at the name of Jesus every knee should bow, of those in heaven, and those on earth, and those under the earth, and that every tongue should confess that Jesus Christ is Lord"* (Phil. 2:9 to 11). After the Wise Men had worshipped Jesus, their gifts were presented to the Child.

I am reminded of another verse that says, *"But without faith it is impossible to please Him, for he who comes to God must believe that He is, and that He is a rewarder of those who diligently seek Him"* (Heb. 11:6). The Wise Men seeking the Saviour, Joseph and Mary faithfully seeking to do the will of God, all received rewards for their diligence.

The trumpets, according to Numbers 10:2-10, were used to summon the people or to warn of battle and the approaching of the enemy. It was a plea to God for deliverance. Those who have accepted Jesus Christ as their Lord and Saviour, at the sounding of the trumpet, when Christ returns to gather His own, will be delivered from this world. *"Behold, I tell you a mystery: We shall not all sleep, but we shall be changed, in a moment, in the twinkling of an eye, at the last trumpet. For the trumpet will sound, and the dead will be raised incorruptible, and we shall be changed"* (1Cor. 15:52).

The Feast of Trumpets depicts the return of Christ and the judgement of the world. Those who have been found faithful will be judged for what they had completed in their life. Crowns will be rewarded for faithfully fulfilling the revealed will of God. These crowns will be presented to Jesus, the Christ at Yon Kippur.

We need to ask the question, 'How long did the Wise Men's journey from Jerusalem take?' Travelling from

Jerusalem to Nazareth, setting up camp, worshipping and spending time with Jesus' family, and some downtime before making the trek home. Would ten days seem, about right? This then brings us to the next feast.

6 Yom Kippur (Day of Atonement)

Tishri 10. September/October. Fall Feast.
Lev. 23:27-36

Yom Kippur, is the most solemn of Jewish religious holidays, observed on the 10th day after the Feast of Trumpets. During this time, Jews seek to make amends for their sins and achieve reconciliation with God. Yom Kippur concludes after the ten days of repentance. The Bible refers to Yom Kippur as a Sabbath, because, even though the holy day may fall on a weekday, it is on Yom Kippur that solemnity and the repentance process for that year is ended, and the work is complete. The purpose of Yom Kippur is to effect individual and collective purification by the practice of forgiveness of the sins of others and by sincere repentance for one's own sins against God. Yom Kippur reveals a great host of people, Jews and Gentiles, who will be saved when Jesus physically returns to earth.

When Leviticus 23:27-36 is read, within Yon Kippur, four different activities are observed by the children of Israel.

1. A Holy Convocation. This was to draw the focus of the people to the altar of divine mercy.
2. Prayer. The people of Israel were to humble their souls (Lev. 23:27).
3. Fasting. This was a day of mourning over their sins (v27).
4. Offerings. A time of sacrifice (v27). If these are not done then they will be cut off (Lev. 23:29).

The next event to happen in Jesus' childhood is the flight into Egypt. So, what are the associated events in Jesus' narrative?

- 1a. The Wise Men are divinely warned in a dream not to return to Herod.
- 1b. Joseph also warned in a dream to take the young child and His mother and flee to Egypt.
- 2. Herod's response.
- 3. Massacre of innocent.
- 4. The parent's response to their loss.

After worshipping the new King, the Wise Men, being divinely warned in a dream they should not return to Herod, departed for their own country another way (Matt. 2:12). Obedience really differentiates between those who worship Jesus and those who refuse. We are always provided with a way of escape when we follow the lead of the Holy Spirit. Obedience and disobedience. Life or death. These were truly Wise Men, for they chose life. Joseph also took the young Child and His mother by night and departed for Egypt (Matt. 2:14).

When Herod ordered boys under two years of age to be slaughtered, the majority of people were not affected. However, the small number of Israelites who had their babies slain, suffered. The families whose children were not killed should have been drawn to and focused on His divine mercy that did not involve them. One would think many prayers along with fasting would have accompanied the loss of children to parents. Certainly, the shedding of innocent blood, a time of sacrifice for some also is relevant here. Herod's actions bought consequences for many. When Jesus returns, His actions will also bring life or death.

The Wise Men giving gifts to Jesus parallels to us giving Jesus our crowns received at the Feast of Trumpets, when the righteous are judged and given rewards for the life they have lived. The scripture says, *"Lay up for yourselves treasures in heaven, where neither moth nor rust destroys and where thieves do not break in and steel"* (Matt. 6:20). The crowns we have received, will be presented to Jesus, for saving us from the Lake of Fire. When we kneel before Jesus, we will know the reality of the words we have sung;

Crown Him with many crowns,
The Lamb upon His throne;
Hark! how the heavenly anthems drowns
All music but its own;
Awake, my soul, and sing
Of Him who died for thee,

And hail Him as thy matchless King
Through all eternity.

So, Jesus' family travels to Egypt at the bidding of God. What awaits them in this place, not of their choosing but God's?

7 *Feast of Tabernacles*

Tishri 15-22. September/October. Fall Feast.
Lev. 23:39, 2 Chron. 8:13, Ezra 3:4, Zech. 14:16

The feast is also known as the 'Feast of Booths'. The feast was celebrated in remembrance of the time the Children of Israel spent in the desert, using temporary dwellings to live in. A temporary hut or booth, called a 'Sukkah' was built outside the main home consisting of three walls made of any material. The roof was to be made so that, on a clear night, the stars could be seen through it. While shelter was provided, the elements needed to be endured, so representing the hardship of those who were called to walk the way God ordained.

Joseph and Mary were required to pack up their home and travel to Egypt where they would live for an unspecified time, in a temporary abode. While many other Jews lived in Egypt and were free to worship God, living in Egypt was not the family home. Their worship and lives would not be the same as the place or surroundings they left. Travelling from

Nazareth in Galilee to Egypt, possibly took them through Jerusalem. This in itself would have been a dangerous road to take. Joseph was not given another option. Neither is the attendance at the third must-attend feast (Deut. 16:16).

Tabernacles refers to the day when the Son of God will tabernacle among men, wipe away every tear, and bring in the 'golden age' that men have dreamed of since time immemorial.

Summary

While I have presented many parallels between the Feasts of Israel and the events in Jesus' childhood, it is really conjecture on my part. Like 'The Tabernacle', the 'Feasts of Israel' are all about Jesus. So why would they not line up?

Deuteronomy 16:16. *Three times a year all your males shall appear before the Lord your God in the place which He chooses: at the Feast of Unleavened Bread, at the Feast of Weeks, and at the Feast of Tabernacles; and they shall not appear before the Lord empty-handed.*

The Passover. Jesus was certainly the sacrificial lamb, born to die for our salvation.

The Feast of Unleavened Bread. Leaven represents sin. Just as leaven was eradicated from the home, so sin needs to be forgiven in our lives. Jesus gave His life freely so we can obtain forgiveness, enables us to receive eternal life. The 'Feast of Unleavened Bread' was the first must-attend feast, so we need to ask for forgiveness. If we don't attend the feast and ask for forgiveness, we are doomed for eternity.

The Feast of Fruitfruits. Jesus was the first to be raised to new life. We can also have confidence, we too will be raised to new life having asked for forgiveness.

The Feast of Weeks or Pentecost. Just as Jesus was presented at the Temple, we also need to open ourselves to what God wants and requires of us. It is only when we have the power of the Holy Spirit can we live God's will for our lives. Attendance is not an option, as 'Pentecost' is the second must-attend feast.

The Feast of Trumpets. Having attended the second must-attend feast, the Holy Spirit gives us gifts or power to live our life, suited to each of us in His time. Just as Joseph and Mary, the disciples at Pentecost, had no idea about what Father God desires were for them, we don't know what gifts will be granted us or when they will arrive. We just need to be ready to receive them with thanks.

Yom Kippur. It is possible there will be those who will be jealous of what gifts we have received, and will try to bring us down or do us harm. We are told to expect various trials

(James. 1:2). It is only by prayer, fasting and sacrifice will we find ourselves enveloped in the love of God. *"Draw near to God and He will draw near to you"* (James 4:8). Only those who persevere, with persistence and patience, will be counted faithful. As we have completed the revealed will of God, we will be able to bring our offering to Father God and present them to Jesus Christ, His Son.

The Feast of Tabernacles or Booths. It is only in our obedience to God will we find the true path selected for us to walk. Whilst at times we are taken out of our comfort zone, God will not only direct our steps (Prov. 3:6), but also supply all we need for our journey (Phil. 4:19). While it may feel like we have been abandoned at times, God has promised to *'Never leave you nor forsake you'* (Heb. 13:5b). While we live here on earth, we need to be mindful it is only a temporary dwelling that will someday be replaced with a new dwelling. *"Therefore, if anyone is in Christ, he is a new creation; old things have passed away; behold, all things have become new"* (2Cor. 5:17). The 'Feast of Tabernacles' is the third must-attend feast. Having attended both the others, our future hope of the feast of tabernacles, should follow.

A Timeline of God's Ordained Feasts: with the Events of Jesus' Birth

The various accounts throughout the New Testament regarding the Announcement to Mary, about Her being chosen as the one to bear the Messiah, the conception date along with His birth, are all preordained by God, with regard to Jewish history and events.

The year of our Saviour's birth, Jesus Christ, is obscured because there is no conclusive date for Herod's death. Rather than try to prove a date, I will look at the seasons. While years can vary, seasons remain stable. I have accepted Christ's birth as the Passover. Passover was in late March or early April, and is the season of Spring in the Holy Land.

Each event in Christ's birth, is linked to one of the Feasts of Israel which leads to a clear path to follow. The first record of a Christian celebration of Christ's birth was recorded in Spring, of AD 250 in Jerusalem. The first recorded date of

Christmas being celebrated on December 25th was in AD 336, during the time of the Roman Emperor Constantine.

The Christmas date was borrowed from pagan celebrations. The Romans had their mid-winter Saturnalia festival in late December, worshipping Mithras, the god of light. In AD 274, the Roman Emperor Aurelian established a feast of the birth of Sol Invictus, the unconquered Sun god, on December 25. Christmas is really a pagan solar festival. Early Christians deliberately chose the date to encourage the spread of Christianity throughout the Roman world. If Christmas looked like a pagan holiday, more pagans would be open to both the holiday and the God whose birth it celebrated. This would change only after Constantine converted to Christianity. From the mid-fourth century on, we find Christians deliberately adapting and Christianizing pagan festivals. As the Christians believed Jesus' birth was the true God of light, this date was established.

The early Christians were right, as the shepherds, being in the field watching over their sheep, tells me the time was not winter but most likely spring. Spring time in Jerusalem is late March to early June. It is an interesting fact that 'Passover' is celebrated in late March, early April. The feast is all about the sacrificial lamb being slain for the Exodus from Egypt and slavery. Jesus was God's Lamb, ordained to be the Sacrificial

Lamb, whose blood would be shed for the sins of the world. We can then claim that Jesus' birth and death, might very well have been at the same time of year.

We need to work through the events in Mary's life regarding the birth of the promised Messiah. To establish the timeline, we need to go backwards from the birth to the announcement of the angel to Mary. So, let's put them in order. There was the birth of Jesus (Luke 2:6 to 7), the conception (Luke 1:35), Elizabeth's baby jumping in her womb when Mary visited her (Luke 1:41), the announcement by the angel Gabriel to Mary about her being selected to give birth to the Messiah (Luke 1:26 to 38), to see a wonderful hidden sequent of events, masterly planned by the Master Planner.

1 The Birth of Jesus

I chose late March or early April for the birth of the Saviour. As we work back from this date, we can identify the time of conception. A pregnancy is forty weeks, and as we believe, while God can and does use miracles to achieve His revealed will when required, He is also a God who works through the natural things and nature which He created. We can then accept; Mary's term of pregnancy would be around forty weeks. As we travel back in time, we are brought to a date, mid-June. What is a significant feast in the Jewish calendar associated with mid-June?

2 *The Conception*

We need to read a verse associated with an event in Mary's life. Luke has recorded for us, *"And the angel answered and said to her, 'The Holy Spirit will come upon you, and the power of the Highest will overshadow you; therefore, also that Holy One who is to be born will be called the Son of God'"* (Luke 1:35). Are we familiar with another event that happened later, when the Holy Spirit descended upon a group of people gathered in an upper room? When the sound of a rushing mighty wind and tongues of fire descended and rested on each of them and they were changed (Acts 2:1-4)?

The date, mid-June is known as Shavuot or the Feast of Weeks or as we now refer to it as 'Pentecost'. So, what is significant about the feast? Shavuot is celebrated seven days after the second Passover Seder and is one of the three pilgrimage festivals or must-attend feasts (Deut. 16:16). This feast is an ancient grain harvest festival but also identified in Biblical times with the giving of the Torah on Mt. Sinai. Traditionally, the Book of Ruth is read, which conveys greenery and flowers. These are often used to decorate homes during Shavuot because Mount Sinai was thought to have burst into bloom in anticipation of God's word. Considering the preceding passage, would June be an acceptable time for the conception of Jesus, the Son of God?

Reflecting on these two events, the 'Feast of Weeks' and the 'conception' of Jesus, what is apparent? God gave the Hebrews the Law at Sinai, but with the birth of His Son, God gave a redemption plan for lost mankind through Jesus, who would be the Sacrificial Lamb, slain for the sins of the world. It was Saint Augustine who said, 'The New is in the Old concealed, but the Old is in the New revealed'. The Old Testament was all about the law. God was now saying, *"It is by grace you will be saved through faith, and that not of yourselves; it is the gift of God, not of works, lest anyone should boast"* (Eph. 2:8). We are moving from the Law to Grace.

The Jewish people consume dairy foods, including milk, at Shavuot. We're talking about the birth of a child and the care a mother brings to her child through feeding, supplying all the needs at this time in its life. Reading from the Book of Ruth is about a special person used by God to carry out His revealed will. Unlike Mary, Ruth was chosen from outside the covenant people. One would need to ask the question, why was it necessary for God to go outside His favoured people to find someone obedient? The common link for me between these two ladies is obedience. Greenery speaks to me of Spring and new life. What was the Passover time when Jesus was born? Spring. New life, and a new way of living: for those who accept and follow the revealed plan for their life.

3 *Elizabeth's Baby Jumping in Her Womb*

Let us look at the next event, Mary's visit to Elizabeth (Luke 1:39-45, 56). To ascribe an appropriate date when

Mary visited Elizabeth, one would want to align the visit with one of the Major feasts. The first one that comes to mind is Passover as Jesus was to be the Sacrificial Lamb, but would this work? We need to read the scripture to find any clues given to us regarding this event. I was once told, the best reference tool to the Bible is the Bible. That advice made sense then, and makes sense now.

My Bible tells me, *"And Mary remained with her about three months, and returned to her house"* (Luke 1:56).

I also read, *"Blessed is she who believed, for there will be a fulfilment of those things which were told her from the Lord"* (Luke 1:45). This was Elizabeth's prophecy about Mary's future. What was Mary told? *"The Holy Spirit would come upon her and she would be with child. The Holy Spirit would protect her in the days to come, and the One who is to be born will be called the Son of God"* (v35). We know that Mary's stay was three months after she prophesied over her. After three months, and when the 'Feast of Weeks' had passed, Mary returned to her home. Another question is now asked as to what other major significant feasts occurred prior to this date and was relevant to her situation?

4 *The Announcement by the Angel Gabriel to Mary*

As I read my Bible, another substantial clue appears. The verse reads, *"Now in the sixth month the angel Gabriel was sent by God to a city of Galilee named Nazareth to a virgin betrothed to a man whose name was Joseph, of the house of David. The virgin's name was Mary"* (Luke 1:26). I ask the question, what is the sixth month? In the Hebrew calendar the month is 'Tevet', December to January. What other major feast is held at this significant time? Only one comes to mind. The 'Feast of Dedication', the 'Festival of Lights' or 'Hanukah' as we know it today. Is this relevant?

What else do we know? Another verse says, *"Now indeed, Elizabeth your relative has conceived a son in her old age; and this is now the sixth month for her who is called barren"*

Another verse is presented which says, *"Now after those days his wife Elizabeth conceived; and she hid herself five months"* (Luke 1:24). The obvious question is: what is referred to as 'those days'? For the answer to the question we need to look at the story pertaining to the birth of John to Zacharias and Elizabeth.

Luke records, *"So it was, that while he (Zacharias) was serving as priest before God in the custom of the priesthood, his lot fell to burn incense when he went into the temple of the Lord. Then the angel of the Lord appeared to him, standing on the right side of the alter of incense"* (Luke 1:8-9, v11). What significance does this duty have to do with the announcement to Zacharias?

Levitical law states, *"He shall take a censer full of burning coals of fire from the altar before the Lord, with his hands full of sweet incense beaten fine, and bring it inside the veil. And he shall put the incense on the fire before the Lord, that the cloud of incense may cover the mercy seat that is on the Testimony, lest he die"* (Leviticus 16:12-13). The event referred to only happened once a year, on the 'Day of Atonement' or 'Yom Kippur'. Ten days had passed from the 'Feast of Trumpets' before the most Holy Day was celebrated. Gabriel stood on the right side of the altar of incense and revealed to Zacharias the promise of a son to himself and Elizabeth.

The word of God says, *"So it was, as soon as the days of his service were completed, that he departed to his own house. Now after those days his wife Elizabeth conceived"* (Luke 1:1:23-24a). We can now accept that the announcement occurred on 'Yom Kippur' and a few days later, being the 'Feast of Tabernacles' Elizabeth conceived. The relevance of the feast aligns with John's life, as the children of Israel spent forty years in the hardship conditions of the desert or wilderness, so John spent his time living in the deserts till the day of his manifestation to Israel (Luke 1:80).

As we have established the announcement and conception of John to Zacharias and Elizabeth, the announcement to Mary can be established. We are told in scripture, *"Now indeed, Elizabeth your relative has conceived a son in her old age; and this is now the sixth month for her who is called barren"* (Luke 1:36). In her sixth month was more than six months but not seven. 'Passover' is more than six months but not seven from the 'Feast of Tabernacles'.

Let's summarise what we have discovered. Gabriel appeared to Zacharias on 'Yon Kippur'. A few day later on the 'Feast of Tabernacles', Elizabeth conceived John. Gabriel appeared to Mary at Passover and told her she had found favour with God, and would conceive a child by the Holy Spirit. He would be the Son of God. Although Mary did not understand what was going to happen, Mary agreed to be obedient when the Angel explained things to her. Her response to the angel was, *"Behold the maidservant of the Lord! Let it be to me according to your word"* (Luke 1:38). Being encouraged by her Aunt Elizabeth, she became obedient to the revealed will of God. During the Feast of Weeks, the conception with Mary and the Holy Spirit took place. Under the protection of God, Mary had the abiding presence through all these times. Forty weeks later, being Passover, Mary gave birth to a son, *"And you shall call His name Jesus, for He shall save His people from their sin. And they called His name Immanuel, which translated, God with us"* (Matthew 1:21, 23).

The Accepted, Traditional, Christmas Story

When Mary was engaged to Joseph, an angel appeared to her. The angel Gabriel told Mary she was going to be made pregnant by God and would have His Son. Mary was told by the angel to call Him 'Emanuel'. Joseph was not pleased when Mary shared with him what the angel had told her. Joseph wanted to call off the engagement, but the angel told Joseph to marry Mary as this was what God wanted.

Not long before the baby was to be born, Caesar Augustus declared a census. Everyone was required to travel to their own city. Joseph, with his betrothed pregnant Mary, set out for Bethlehem, with Mary riding on a donkey.

When the couple arrived at Bethlehem, there were no rooms available in the whole town. It was at the last place, where the Innkeeper offered them a place in his stable occupied by the animals. Joseph and Mary accepted his offer and the baby Jesus was born in a stable surrounded by animals.

Out on the hillside, an angel appeared to some shepherds who were minding their sheep, and told them about the birth of Jesus. They were afraid and crouched on the ground. The angel told them they would find a baby wrapped in swaddling cloths lying in a manger in Bethlehem. Then a heavenly host of angels filled the night-sky with singing. When this was over, the shepherds decided they should go quickly to Bethlehem and see if what they had been told was true. They found Joseph and Mary with the baby Jesus in a manger, just as the angel said.

Wise Men or Kings from the east had gone to the palace to look for the new born king, because they had seen His star in the east and had followed it all the way to Jerusalem. Herod asked the priests to explain what they knew. The priests told him the king was born in Bethlehem. Herod told the Wise Men to go to Bethlehem. He also suggested they return and tell him where they found the baby king, so he could go and worship.

When the Wise Men left the palace, the star continued on and led them to Bethlehem, where in a stable, the Wise Men were able to worship the new born king and present Him with their gifts of Gold, Frankincense and Myrrh. The angel told these men not to return to Herod, but to go home another way.

When the Wise Men or Kings did not return, Herod had all the male babies under two years of age killed. Joseph was also told in a dream to go and live in Egypt until it was safe to return home.

I struggled to write the preceding account of the event as this is what the world in general accepts happened. How far has the truth been removed from the story should become evident when the real facts are all known and put into place. While many will continue in their own beliefs as to the story, those who are in touch with Father God and the Holy Spirit; will appreciate the underlining facts, as this adds so much more to the understanding of the event.

Hidden Lessons in The Christmas Story

Introducing Mary and Her Family

God chose Mary, a young woman living in Nazareth to be the mother of His Son Jesus. What do we know about Mary?

Mary lived with her parents, and her sister Salome, and as members of the tribe of Judah, they worshipped Yahweh.

Before we proceed, we need to establish the link between Mary and Salome.

The apostle John writes, *"Now their stood by the cross of Jesus His mother, and His mother's sister, Mary the wife of Clopas, and Mary Magdalene"* (John 19:25a).

Matthew writes, *"And many women followed Jesus from Galilee. Mary Magdalene, Mary the mother of James and Joses, and the mother of Zebedee's sons"* (Matt. 27:55-56).

Mark writes, *"Mary Magdalene. Mary the mother of James the Less and of Joses, and Salome"* (Mark 15:40).

From these verses, Salome can be identified as, the mother of Zebedee's children, James and John, and the sister of Jesus' mother Mary. Salome was an Aunt to Jesus and James and John were Jesus' cousins.

Mary's Betrothal

Mary was only in her teen years and was betrothed. His name was Joseph and he was a carpenter. Joseph and his parents also belonged to the tribe of Judah.

What did it mean to be 'Betrothed' in Biblical times? In ancient times, marriage was looked upon as more of an alliance for reasons of survival or practicality. The concept of romantic love remained a secondary issue if considered at all. Romantic love was expected to grow within the marriage. It was the custom for the groom's parents to arrange a marriage, however, the bride's consent to the marriage was an important consideration. Rebecca, for example, was asked if she agreed to go back with Abraham's servant to marry Abraham's son, Isaac. She went willingly (Gen. 24:57–59). During the betrothal time, the groom was to prepare a place for his bride, while the bride focused on her personal preparations: wedding garments, lamps, etc.

Although the bride knew to expect her groom after about a year from the day she accepted the marriage proposal, she did not know the exact day or hour. He could come earlier.

It was the father of the groom who gave final approval for him to return to collect his bride. For this reason, the bride kept her oil lamps ready at all times, just in case the groom came in the night, sounding the shofar to lead the bridal procession to the home he had prepared for her.

The Angel's Visit to Mary

An angel told Mary she was going to become pregnant and have a baby boy by the Holy Spirit, not by her betrothed husband-to-be, Joseph. Mary could not understand how such a thing could happen. The angel, Gabriel, assured her, she had found favour with God, and He had chosen her to give birth to His Son. The angel Gabriel told Mary that when the Child was born, she was to call Him Jesus. This name meant, *'Emanuel'* or *'God with us'.*

Luke records, *"Elizabeth, your relative, has also conceived a son in her old age"* (Luke 1:36a).

Who is Elizabeth?

Who are Elizabeth and Zacharias? We require a little supposition for us to understand their relationship with Mary.

The gospel of Luke says that Mary and Elizabeth were kin. But how were they related?

Elizabeth is John the Baptist's mother and we are told that she was considered old, beyond the age of childbearing. Thus, there was a considerable age difference between both Elizabeth and Mary.

Is it likely they were from different generations but related in some way? Could Elizabeth have had a sister who married a man from the tribe of Judah? This would make Elizabeth a relative and an Aunt to Mary.

Num. 36:6-7 implies that the purpose of the laws forbidding intermarriage between tribes was to prevent loss of inheritance.

[6] This is what the Lord commands concerning the daughters of Zelophehad, saying,
'Let them marry whom they think best,
but they may marry only within the family of their father's tribe.'
[7] So the inheritance of the children of Israel shall not change hands from tribe to tribe,
for every one of the children of Israel shall keep the inheritance of the tribe of his fathers.

The Levites did not own nor inherit anything because they belonged to the Lord. It's possible that Mary's mother was of Levitical heritage, and related to Elizabeth's family, while Mary's father was from Judah, therefore passing on the tribal identification to his daughter.

It seems reasonable to accept; Elizabeth and Mary's mother were sisters. Elizabeth would therefore be Mary's Aunt.

Zacharias was a Levite and so was his wife Elizabeth (Luke 1:5). We are told that Zacharias and Elizabeth were both well advanced in years (Luke 1:7). To estimate their ages, we need to consult the Levitical Law about priests because Zacharias was a priest. It is written, *"At the age of fifty years, the priests must cease performing service, and shall work no more"* (Num. 8:24-26). From this, we understand anyone carrying out priestly duties was under the age of fifty. Once retired from the official priestly duties, the priests were forbidden to do any sacrificial work. Their duties were now of support to the officiating Priests. Scripture tells us that Elizabeth and Zacharias were considered advanced in years and Elizabeth was beyond childbearing. However, Zacharias must have been younger than fifty.

Mary's Uncle, Zacharias, had been visited by the angel Gabriel, when carrying out his Priestly duties in the temple. The angel Gabriel told him his wife Elizabeth was going to have a baby. Because they had never had any children, they were delighted. The angel told him, that when the baby was born, they were to call him John. As Zacharias questioned what the angel Gabriel had told him, he was struck mute until the baby was born.

Zacharias Meets the Angel Gabriel.

Zacharias was carrying out his duty burning incense in the Temple (Luke 1:8-9). Incense was burnt regularly at the 'Incense Altar', which was in the main part of the temple along with the Candelabra, and the Shew Bread Table.

When reading the scripture associated with the event, we gain a greater appreciation of what had occurred.

"Once a year, on the Day of Atonement, coals from the altar were taken in a censer, or fire holder with two handfuls of incense, into the Holy of Holies, where the incense was made to smoke before the mercy seat of the ark of the testimony" (Lev. 16:12-13).

Zacharias was in the Holy of Holies, which the allotted Priest entered once each year. The heavy curtain separated the two parts. He had taken live coals from the 'Brazen Altar', along with two handfuls of incense, to burn before the 'Ark of Testimony', covering the Ark with smoke. When he emerged, Zacharias saw Gabriel standing at the right side of the 'Incense Altar'. Gabriel had appeared to Zacharias on the holiest of days, 'Yom Kippur'. Gabriel, standing next to the 'Incense Altar', shared with Zacharias, that his wife Elizabeth would and have a baby, they were to name him John, and he would be filled with the Holy Spirit in the womb.

Mary Visits Elizabeth

Even though Mary accepted the angel's news, she was a little confused about the details and the implications for her future. Mary thought she should visit her Aunt Elizabeth and Uncle Zacharias. Maybe they could explain more about the visitation of the angel, as Levites were educated in spiritual matters.

Elizabeth was filled with joy when her niece Mary arrived. Mary told Elizabeth she had been chosen by God to give birth to the long-awaited Messiah. We are told, *"When Elizabeth heard the greeting of Mary, the babe leaped in her womb; and Elizabeth was filled with the Holy Spirit"* (Luke 1:41). Gabriel had previously told Zacharias that John, the baby boy they were to conceive, would *"be filled with the Holy Spirit, even from his mother's womb"* (Luke 1:15b).

Elizabeth was so overcome with Mary's news, she burst into prophecy over Mary. *"Blessed are you among women, and blessed is the fruit of your womb!"* (Luke 1:42), and *"Blessed is she who believed, for there will be fulfilment of those things which were told you from the Lord"* (Luke 1:45).

Mary remained with her relatives for about three months; the question is why? Did Mary stay to support Elizabeth in the home duties and general care? Zacharias would then be free to attend the temple and carry out his priestly duties without the concern for his wife.

I am sure Elizabeth and Mary would have spent much time in prayer and discussion during Mary's stay. Encouraged by her relatives, Mary burst into a song of praise to Glorify God. (Luke 1:46-55)

"My soul magnifies the Lord,
And my spirit has rejoiced in God my Saviour.

For He has regarded the lowly state of His maidservant;
For behold, henceforth all generations will call me blessed.
For He who is mighty has done great things for me,
And holy is His name.
And His mercy is on those who fear Him
From generation to generation.
He has shown strength with His arm;
He has scattered the proud in the imagination of their hearts.
He has put down the mighty from their thrones,
And exalted the lowly.
He has filled the hungry with good things,
And the rich He has sent away empty.
He has helped His servant Israel,
In remembrance of His mercy,
As He spoke to our fathers,
To Abraham and to his seed forever."

The time had come for Mary to return home to Nazareth.

Mary Tells Joseph Her News and His Response

When Mary told Joseph she was pregnant, he did not know what to do. Mary being pregnant in this time of betrothal, was not something Joseph found easy to accept. He thought it was best to break off the engagement. But an angel visited Joseph and assured him, the pregnancy was the will of God, and he was to marry Mary (Matt. 1:18-25). Joseph was obedient to the known will of God and eventually married his betrothed wife, but not until she had brought forth that which was Holy to the Lord (Luke 2:5-7).

As I read the account about Joseph, and his decision-making, it appears he had three courses of action.

Firstly, he could break off the engagement, and make Mary a very public spectacle. This would lay the complete blame at the feet of Mary, and she would be found guilty of adultery. She would be humiliated in front of all those who knew her, including her parents being humiliated, which would have bought disgrace to the family. Then she would have been stoned to death. Joseph was a 'Just Man', and his reasoning about Mary's condition demonstrates his maturity. If their marriage was arranged, Joseph could have been some years older than Mary. His mature response showed the love he had for his betrothed bride Mary. Joseph was within his right to divorce Mary according to Levitical law. *"When a man takes a wife and marries her, and he finds some uncleanness in her, he can write a certificate of divorce, put it in her hand and send her out of his house"* (Deut. 24:1). Joseph could have thought Mary's pregnancy as being unclean, because the child was conceived out of wedlock. Because the conception was by the Holy Spirit, no contamination or blemish was present in any way, shape or form.

Secondly, Joseph could put her away quietly. This meant Joseph would share the responsibility with Mary. No public spectacle was made, but she would live and have the baby without Joseph's support.

Thirdly, choosing to marry Mary; meant Joseph would accept full responsibility for Mary and her baby, even though he had committed no sin and was not the father of the child. Such was his love for his betrothed; Joseph did not hesitate to obey the command of God, delivered by the angel.

Parallels between Joseph's response and Jesus coming for His bride

There is a great underlying lesson in Joseph's response to Mary's situation. Just as Joseph accepted full responsibility for Mary's condition, and covered the situation of his betrothed wife-to-be, Jesus accepted full responsibility for our sin. I see Joseph is so much like Jesus. Jesus could have taken the first option to let the world and the people within, die in their sins. But He didn't. Jesus could have compelled people to share the responsibility for their sin by keeping the Law, which was the second option. But He didn't. Jesus chose to die for our sins, taking the full responsibility for our sin. The love that Father God has for us, His children, through Jesus is giving us life, whereas we actually deserve death.

When Father God declares all things are ready, Jesus will return to claim His bride, the Church. Although the Church is mostly unfaithful to Him, there is a remnant within the church that has remained faithful. This aligns with the teaching about the sheep and goats (Matt. 25:31-46). The main body of the church are represented by goats; the remnant as sheep. Mary was the favoured one. Jesus, in His teaching said, *"Many are called but few are choice"* (Matt. 22:14). While many were called to be the children of Israel, Mary was a choice one, called to a special task by God. Mary was part of the remnant. When Jesus returns to usher His own into eternity; the sins of the remnant are covered by the shed blood of Jesus. Even though He was without sin, *"He made Him who knew no sin to be sin for us, that we might become the righteousness of God in Him"* (2Cor. 5:21).

Joseph did not marry Mary until the promised Child of God was born. We read, *"Joseph was of the house and lineage of David, to be registered with Mary, his betrothed wife, who was with child"* (Luke 2:4-5). It was not until their return to Nazareth (Luke 2:39), the wedding took place (Matt. 1:25). While the betrothal time would normally be around one year for the groom to come for his bride, Joseph and Mary's betrothal would have been in the vicinity of eighteen months. One could imagine people saying to Mary, 'What is the delay? He should have been here to get you all ready'. While Mary knew the love Joseph had for her, she waited patiently for his coming, because she trusted Joseph. Many today are saying, *"Where is the promise of His coming? For since the fathers fell asleep, all things continue as they were from the beginning of creation"* (2Peter 3:4). We as believers know Jesus' delay in coming for His bride, the church, will only happen after all things have been accomplished. Jesus gave clear instructions to His disciples about His return, for He said, *"This generation will not pass away until all things shall have taken place"* (Matt. 24:34).

The Roman Census

While Mary was preparing for the birth of God's Son, devastating news came that Joseph was required to travel to Bethlehem, to be registered. Caesar Augustus, the Emperor, had decreed all people should be registered, and everyone was required to travel to his own city of origin.

The census imposed by the Emperor would most likely not include women, just the male heads of the household. Joseph and Mary choosing to make this journey together, fulfils Biblical prophecies, although it is only hindsight that opens prophecy to us. Micah prophesied (Micah 5:2),

"But you, Bethlehem, in the land of Judah,
are not the least among the rulers of Judah;
For out of you shall come a Ruler
Who will shepherd My people
Israel."

The Bible tells us, *"Joseph with his betrothed wife, who was with child"* (Luke 2:5). The Holy Spirit was active, and

God's chosen people were being prompted in ways that were not usual. First, there was Zacharias with Elizabeth giving birth to a son. Then there was Mary, who was told she would conceive and give birth to the long-awaited Messiah. Joseph, a just man, a man of faith, obediently obeyed what the angel told him to do. What we need to remember is that God had been silent for four hundred years.

The Journey to Bethlehem

As the journey would have taken four to five days, it is most likely, Joseph would have allowed sufficient time for his pregnant wife-to-be, to be comfortable during the journey. We need to remember that God had promised Mary would be overshadowed by the power of the Highest (Luke 1:35). As they were poor, Joseph and Mary would have travelled by donkey. As they travelled in spring, temperatures during the daytime could be hot, but not as hot as summer days. Joseph would have walked as he led the donkey, carefully selecting a smooth path for the donkey's feet. This would have given comfort to Mary as she rode.

The Family Members

What we need to address is, how many were in the family group who travelled from Nazareth to Bethlehem. During their betrothal, Mary and Joseph would have been living with their respective families. As both families were from the tribe of Judah, it is safe to infer they would have all been travelling to Bethlehem for the census. It is then reasonable to think there were at least six people in this party. Joseph and Mary may have chosen to stay with Zacharias and Elizabeth longer in Jerusalem, while the others went on to Bethlehem, to spend time with the other relatives waiting and living there. Joseph and Mary staying with Zacharias, Elizabeth and John when they arrived at Jerusalem; would give Mary a well-earned rest. The importance of this visit will be revealed later.

Who Are Jacob and Heli?

Two verses are required to understand the relationship between Joseph and Mary.

Matthew records, *"And Jacob begot Joseph the husband of Mary, of whom was born Jesus who is called Christ"* (Matt. 1:16).

Luke records, *"Now Jesus Himself began His ministry at about thirty years of age, being (as was supposed) the son of Joseph, the son of Heli"* (Luke 3:23).

Both Matthew and Luke outline the genealogy of Jesus Christ. Matthew traces the lineage of Jesus from Abraham through Joseph, although he is careful to point out Joseph was not Jesus' actual father (Matt. 1:18). His purpose, since he was writing for a Jewish audience, was to prove that Jesus was the promised Messiah. Matthew named Jacob as the father of Joseph.

Luke ascends the family line all the way to Adam, therefore identifying Jesus universally with the human race.

Matthew chose the legal line of descent through Joseph, where Luke gave the lineage of Mary, the only human parent of Jesus. Luke named Heli as the father of Mary.

Accommodation in Bethlehem

Bethlehem was a very small village and the inhabitants would have known each other. Many of them would have been related and as was the custom of the day, visiting relations would share the family home. The biblical recount of Joseph and Mary's arrival in Bethlehem states that there was no room in the Inn. We need to understand the real meaning of the word 'Inn'. The word 'Inn' is only used twice in the New Testament. The first time Luke uses the word Inn, *'kataluma'*, meaning a guest room (Luke 2:7). The second time Luke uses the word Inn, *'pandokheion'*, meaning a commercial inn used for travellers (Luke 10:34).

What Luke is really saying, is that when Joseph and Mary finally arrived at their destination, the guest room was occupied with visiting relatives. They were offered a part of the living area where the resident family slept and ate. Within the same room, there was an area where the domestic animals were housed in the winter months. Because the time was spring, no animals were using this area. Joseph and Mary were more than happy to use this area normally used for the livestock, as Mary and Joseph would still have privacy, and when the time came, the other women who were family, would give support with the birth.

Typical village home in Bethlehem

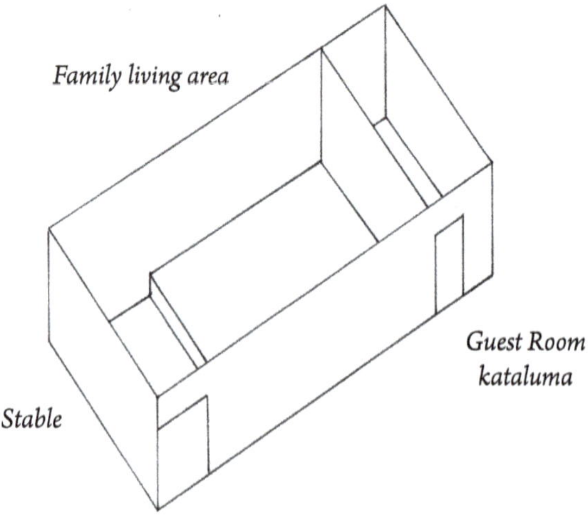

God had centuries to get ready for the birth of His Son, Jesus Christ. Seven hundred years before the birth of Jesus, the prophet Micah prophesied that the Messiah would be born in Bethlehem.

"You, O Bethlehem Ephrathah, who are too little to be among the clans of Judah, from you shall come forth for me one who is to be ruler in Israel, whose coming forth is from of old, from ancient days" (Micah 5:2)

God had seven hundred years to plan the details of the incarnation of His Son to be born in the right place, at the right time, and in the right way. God could easily arrange that a just man and a faithful virgin, in the lineage of David, would be living in Bethlehem in accordance with the prophecy. But God chose Mary and Joseph, who lived in Nazareth, not Bethlehem. God planned for Mary to get pregnant far from the prophesied town and sent an angel to tell her.

To solve the problem which God Himself created, He could have arranged for Joseph and Mary to be in Bethlehem by some personal means, as a relative who needed them urgently or a dream. But He didn't. God moved Joseph and Mary from Nazareth to Bethlehem by creating an empire-wide census. In other words, God arranged that the most powerful leader in the world would order everyone in his empire, to go to the town of their origin to register.

God was making a point. He orchestrated events exactly the way He planned, including the birth of His Son. It may appear ridiculous to think, that a God who moves an empire to move one woman from Nazareth to Bethlehem, can't arrange a guest room. Planning a bed for His Son was easier than planning a global census. Jesus was lying in exactly the place God planned, a feeding trough.

The Feast of Unleavened Bread and the Cleansing of the Place of Jesus' birth

The day before 'Passover' is called the 'Day of Preparation'. Every Jewish home was cleaned from top to bottom and any leaven was removed as leaven represented sin.

Jesus being born on Passover, meant the environment, the place where He would be born, would be spotless, not a filthy dirty stable with animals, somewhere outside the home. The spotless Lamb of God was born into the world, in an area that had been cleansed of anything that might resemble sin. Because Jesus was born of the Holy Spirit, meaning He had an earthly mother and the Holy Spirit as His Father, He was born without the tendency to sin, as this tendency is inherited to all of us through our earthly father.

Jesus is Born. Swaddling Cloths and the Manager

When Jesus was born He was wrapped in swaddling cloths and laid in a manger. The significance of these two events will become apparent in the next section of the text.

The Shepherds

The church historian Eusebius linked the Shepherds' Fields outside Bethlehem, to a unique biblical location called Migdal Eder, which translated means the 'Tower of the Flock'. The lambs were raised for use in temple sacrifices as well as for Passover. The Passover lambs had to be one-year-old and without spot or blemish. Micah 4: 8 says,

And you, O tower of the flock,
The stronghold of the daughter of Zion,
To you shall it come,
Even the former dominion shall come,
The kingdom of the daughter of Jerusalem.

Prominent Jewish writers concluded in the Midrash that from all of the places in Israel, it would be the Migdal Eder where the arrival of the Messiah would be declared first.

Unbeknown to Mary, Father God was also celebrating the birth of His Son. He sent an Angel to tell some temple trainee shepherds, who were looking after the spotless lambs for the sacrifices in some nearby pastures, that the Saviour of the world had been born in Bethlehem. They would find a baby wrapped in swaddling cloths and lying in a manger. The shepherds were so afraid; they crouched on the ground. But then, a multitude of the heavenly hosts began to sing,

"Glory to God in the highest, and on earth peace, goodwill toward men" (Luke 2:14).

And then, as quick as the angel and the heavenly hosts arrived, they were gone.

My thoughts are trying to process why an angel chorus would sing to shepherd priests? Was there a hidden message in this event? Observing a prompting of the Holy Spirit, I turned to the scriptures and in particular to Psalm 150.

Praise the Lord!
Praise God in His sanctuary;
Praise Him in His mighty firmament!

2 Praise Him for His mighty acts;
Praise Him according to His excellent greatness!
3 Praise Him with the sound of the trumpet;
Praise Him with the lute and harp!
4 Praise Him with the timbrel and dance;
Praise Him with stringed instruments and flutes!
5 Praise Him with loud cymbals;
Praise Him with clashing cymbals!
6 Let everything that has breath praise the Lord.
Praise the Lord!

As I look at these words, verses three, four and five, suggest we can use instruments and dance. We don't need to be quiet. We can praise Him loudly! Let us look again to the Psalms for advice concerning our worship. Psalm 100.

Make a joyful shout to the Lord, all you lands!
2 Serve the Lord with gladness;
Come before His presence with singing.
3 Know that the Lord, He is God;
It is He who has made us, and not we ourselves;
We are His people and the sheep of His pasture.
4 Enter into His gates with thanksgiving,
And into His courts with praise.
Be thankful to Him, and bless His name.
5 For the Lord is good;
His mercy is everlasting,
And His truth endures to all generations.

The Holy Spirit will lead and guide us to what is a present, acceptable praise to our God.

This Psalm suggests we can worship God anywhere, and isn't that precisely how the Angel Choir worshipped their Creator? I could image verses one, two and six, befitting the heavenly choir.

But what were the words the Angels sang? *"Glory to God in the highest, and on earth peace, goodwill toward men"* (Luke 2:14). These words pose a question, "What was the angels' message in the words they sang?"

First, and foremost, *'God is to be glorified'.* Sin had dishonoured Him, destroyed His rule and broken the perfect order of His creation. His Son, Jesus Christ was born to redeem the lost and restore man to the place He was formed to be.

Secondly, *'Man is to enjoy peace'.* There is no peace for the wicked, because real peace is only available through the shed blood of Jesus Christ who was born to die for our sins on a cruel cross. Every sinner, who believes in the saving power of the cross, obtains the peace that surpasses all understanding (Phil. 4:7).

Thirdly, *'Goodwill is to reign among men'.* Men are to love one another. The words are a fitting message to those who professed to keep the law. The Angels were proclaiming the truth, *"Old things are passed away; behold, all things have become new"* (2Cor. 5:17). Your days of animal sacrifice are numbered. You're about to become redundant. God has moved from law to grace.

The shepherds were not poor, stinky, and ragtag, as some might presume. A look at Jewish priestly duties explains more about what the shepherds were really like, without destroying the romantic bubble surrounding that first Noel. The shepherds were actually fulfilling Temple duties, and the only ones who could perform Temple duties were priests. We know they were priests because it is recorded in the Mishnah. The Mishnah is a collection of documents that record the oral traditions that governed the Jewish people during the time of the Pharisees. One of its regulations expressly forbids *"the keeping of flocks throughout the land of Israel except in the wilderness, and the only flocks otherwise kept would be those for the Temple services"* (Bab K.7:7; 80a). These shepherds were in the fields surrounding Bethlehem, not out in the wilderness where regular sheep were kept. So, they must have been priests. Why would priests perform menial shepherding duties for the Temple? It's because the sheep were to be sacrificed for Passover. It was the priests' job to make sure the lambs were without blemish and completely unharmed before being sacrificed.

Swaddling Cloths

The Holy Spirit was actively prompting the people involved in the Birth of Jesus, according to the will of Father God.

Each detail must be meticulously carried out. In the area of the family room where the domestic animals would normally be, Mary was prompted to lay her precious Baby wrapped in swaddling cloths in a manager that was normally used to feed the animals during the night. She knew He would be safe, and away from the traffic of the family.

Out in the distant fields, the Angel instructed some temple trainee priest shepherds, *"This will be a sign to you: You will find a Babe wrapped in swaddling cloths, lying in a manger"* (Luke 2:12). How often do we miss the details in the account of Jesus' birth? The Holy Spirit prompted Mary to lay the babe in the manager. The Angel used this detail to help the shepherds find the baby.

But what's so important about swaddling cloths? These weren't ordinary cloths. They weren't rags Mary and Joseph brought from home or happened to find in the home where they were staying. These were the same cloths used by the priests; specifically, the shepherd priests to keep the lambs clean and free of blemishes as the lambs were looked after and prepared for the sacrifice at 'Passover'. How Mary and Joseph acquired these cloths is unknown, but they could have been given to them from the priest, Zacharias, whose wife Elizabeth, Mary's Aunt, gave to them when Mary and Joseph stayed within their home on the way to Bethlehem. Zacharias and Elizabeth would have used swaddling cloths for John when he was born, because he was of the tribe of the Levites. So, the shepherds found baby Jesus wrapped in priestly cloths. Since Jesus is the Lamb of God (John 1:29) and the great High Priest (Heb. 4:14), it's only fitting, because one day He would be sacrificed, an unblemished Lamb for all mankind.

The Manger

Mangers are animal feeding troughs; in ancient Israel they were made of stone. Not comfortable, but great for protection. That's why the priests would put their newborn lambs in these mangers for protection. But not just any lamb, the unblemished perfect lambs that were used to sacrifice for sins. They had to be perfect, so the temple shepherds would wrap them tightly in cloth and lie them in the manger to keep them safe. This is exactly why the only time mangers are mentioned is in Jesus' birth story. The Bible says, *"This will be a sign for you, you will find a baby wrapped in cloth and lying in a manger"* (Luke 2:12). The shepherds should have understood this powerful parallel. They knew what the cloth and the manger meant. This baby would be the perfect Lamb of God. The Messiah: who would sacrifice His life for the sins of the whole world. He wasn't just a baby wrapped in swaddling cloths lying in a manger: He was God, Perfect, Sinless and Holy. He Humbled Himself to become the perfect sacrifice to reconcile us back to Him.

The Shepherd's Visit and Mary's Treasured Memories

The family members were overwhelmed when the shepherds arrived as they had not witnessed the Angelic visit or the Choir of Angels singing, only a short distance from their home. Those in the house listened intently to all the shepherds had to say, as they retold the event over and over. Mary didn't say very much, she just listened and kept all the shepherds had said in her heart.

Mary treasured the memory of each event associated with her Babe's birth, and her list of treasures was growing. How blessed was she to have the angel Gabriel visit her in person. The wisdom of her Uncle and Aunt; had comforted her. How the promise of being overshadowed, had saved her from certain death. Her betrothed, Joseph, loved her deeply, far more than she had imagined. An acceptable place was granted to her by Joseph's family, sharing their own room for her to have God's anointed. And now the shepherds, sharing with her about the angel's announcement to them and God's heavenly host sang praises. How the shepherds were told to look for a baby wrapped in swaddling cloths lying in a manger would be a sign to them. This was an intimate detail that only Mary was aware of, which she was prompted by the Holy Spirit to carry out. No wonder Mary was amazed. Did she wonder at what else her Father God had in mind? Only time would reveal.

What treasured things do we keep in our heart? Maybe more regrets than treasure? My treasured things are gifts of sentimental value as I remember the person, their presence and the influence they had in my life. How Father God daily cares and supplies for me. How Father God reveals secrets to me daily from His word for my edification and spiritual growth. How those who love me unconditionally, share my life. How my writings, guided by the Holy Spirit, bring immense satisfaction to me, and those who choose to read the revealed word. These are a few of my treasured things.

One could imagine the shepherds feasting their eyes on Jesus as He lay in the manger. So much of what they were doing with the unblemished lambs, laying them in mangers for protection, was reminiscent of the babe in the manger, being revealed here right before their eyes. In a few weeks, Simeon, the priest, would also be feasting his eyes on Jesus as He lay in his arms. When we look at Jesus, do we feast on the bread of life? Jesus later said, *"I am the bread of life. He who comes to Me shall never be hungry, and he who believes in Me shall never thirst"* (John 6:35).

When the shepherds left, villagers were up and about. The shepherds told everyone what they had witnessed. How the Angel appeared to them and the Heavenly Hosts sang praises to God in the night. While the village slept, the Saviour of the world was born.

A question begging to be asked is, 'Why did the temple shepherds, and not the common people of lowly status, come to see Jesus?' I remembered that Moses was a shepherd when working for Jethro, tending his flock when God called him to lead the children of Israel out of Egypt (Exodus 3:1). Amos was a shepherd from Tekoa, who was chosen to bring judgement against Israel, because they had turned away from God (Amos. 1:1). David was out minding the sheep when Samuel came to anoint the next king of Israel (1Sam. 16:13). He later became King David, succeeding Saul, in the bloodline of the Messiah. Jesus was known as the Son of David. Were any of these lowly common people?

Jesus' birth was just the beginning of the rejection by the Jews. Whom better than temple shepherds to start the ball rolling? John wrote in his gospel, *"He came to His own, and they did not receive Him"* (John 1:11). All through the life of Jesus, the temple priests and scribes came to see and listen, but never discovered the truth (2Tim. 3:7). While the temple shepherd priests came into the presence of the Saviour of the world, is it not recorded they worshipped Him? Father God had given His Son Jesus a mission. *"For the Son of Man has come to seek and save the lost"* (Matt. 18:11, Luke 19:10). Who were the lost? The Levites who were consumed with the law and the keeping of the multiple parts they had imposed. No wonder they never worshipped the Christ Child.

Mary's Time of Purification

The next day was the first must-attend feast, the 'Feast of Unleavened Bread'. This was the day after 'Passover' so, as we are later told, Joseph would have gone up to Jerusalem, as was his custom (Luke 2:42). Mary was unable to attend as she was in her purification time. This was a forty-day time where she was considered unclean, and was forbidden to touch any hallowed thing, nor come into the sanctuary for the remainder of the time. The fact that Mary was regarded as unclean, tells us the Wise Men did not show up on the night, but was reserved for another time in the future. They would not have come into her home, nor would she have been able to touch their gifts. When the other relatives had left, Joseph and Mary, along with Jesus, would have used the guest room.

Presenting Jesus at the Temple

When the forty days of purification were over, the time came for Joseph and Mary to return home to Nazareth. Fifty days after Passover, came the second must-attend feast, 'The Feast of Weeks', which Joseph and Mary could attend at Jerusalem.

Joseph and Mary took their Son Jesus to the temple, to carry out the requirements set out in the Levitical law (Lev. 12:8). Joseph and Mary were required to offer a sacrifice for the new born. A lamb would be offered in thanksgiving for the safe delivery of their son, or if they could not afford a lamb, two turtledoves or two young pigeons would suffice. Being a poor family, they chose the lesser of the sacrifices; two turtledoves.

I am reminded of the song written so many years later, to secretly teach an underlying meaning of Christmas to Christians. The song is, 'The Twelve Days of Christmas'. A Partridge in a pear tree, referred to Jesus dying on the cross. Two turtle doves referred to the Old and New Testaments. Three French hens referred to the Trinity. Four calling birds referred to the four gospels and Five Golden Rings referred to the Pentateuch, the first five books of the Bible, and so the song continues. Joseph and Mary offering 'Two Turtle Doves', were saying, *"Jesus did not come to destroy the Law or the Prophets. He came to fulfill the Law"* (Matt. 5:17).

Simeon the Priest was at the Temple when Mary and Joseph arrived. Like Zacharias, he was nearing retirement but was prompted to attend the Temple that day (Luke 2:27a). When Simeon was presented with the Christ Child and the offerings, he was overcome with joy, as he recognised the Baby as being the Saviour of mankind. He burst into thanksgiving to God and also prophesied over the Christ Child. After many years had passed, Jesus would say to His disciples, *"For where two or three are gathered together in My name, I am there in the midst of them"* (Matt. 18:20).

Simeons' prayer of thanksgiving astonished Joseph and Mary. Part of Simeon's praise said, *"For my eyes have seen Your salvation which You have prepared before the face of all peoples, a light to bring revelation to the Gentiles, and the glory of Your people Israel"* (Luke 2:20-32). In this last part, Simeon quoted the words of the prophet Isaiah when he wrote, *"I, the Lord, have called You in righteousness, and will hold Your hand; I will keep You and give You as a covenant to the people, as a light to the Gentiles"* (Isaiah. 42:6).

Simeon also foretold of Jesus' destiny and how it would affect Mary later in her life. Jesus' parents did not really understand the prophecy. The fact that, *"A sword will pierce through your own soul also"* (Luke 2:35a), would not be revealed or understood by Mary for another thirty-three years. It was the Holy Spirit at Pentecost, who brought the real revelation of why and what God's Son was born into the world to accomplish.

Anna was also there, a prophetess, who prophesied about this One, to those who looked for redemption in Israel (Luke 2:38, Isa. 9:2, 42:6, 49:6, 60:1-3).

"A light to bring revelation to the Gentiles,
and the glory of Your people Israel."

Just as Simeon had recognised Jesus as the Messiah, the One who would bring redemption to Israel, Anna also prophesied to others of similar persuasion who were looking and waiting for the coming Messiah. There were a group of men living in the east who were also looking for the Messiah. While Joseph and Mary wondered about all these things, neither understood what the Prophesies would mean for them and their family in the future days.

Mary and Joseph Return to Nazareth

After worshipping at the Temple and completing the sacrificial requirements, Joseph, Mary and Jesus returned to Nazareth and the official wedding ceremony.

It was a common custom for the bride to join the groom's father's household, rather than the groom and the bride establishing their own household. So, if the bride and groom were of marriageable age, the groom would return to his father's house after the betrothal to prepare a bridal chamber. This process traditionally took a year or more (the length of time being dictated by the groom's father). When the place was complete, the groom would return and fetch his bride. The bride would not know the day or hour of her husband-to-be's return, so the groom's arrival was usually announced with a trumpet call and a shout so the bride had some forewarning. Later in His teaching ministry, Jesus would use the wedding event to tell about His return. The parable of the 'Wise and Foolish Virgins' (Matt. 25:1-13), leaves us in no doubt, while Jesus has gone to prepare a place for us, we need to be ready for His return, preparing ourselves under the guidance of the Holy Spirit. While the Feasts of Israel have played a major part in past events, one could expect the return would be at the 'Feast of Trumpets' being in September. Peter assures us, we will not know when He will return to gather the faithful, only that He will come as a thief in the night (2Peter 3:10), we just need to be ready.

More Visitors

The unexpected things in life can cause havoc. Other events were taking place that Joseph, Mary and Jesus had no knowledge about. Away in the east, some Wise Men had seen a star that indicated a king was born. The new born king was no ordinary king, as He was born, 'King of the Jews'.

Why would men in the east be looking for a star and a new king, born King of the Jews? It should be noted, when Jesus was born, there were more Jews living outside Jerusalem, dispersed throughout the Roman Empire than there were in Jerusalem. Waves of captivity had taken learned men and boys, such as Daniel, Shadrack, Meshack and Abednego who were princes back in their own country. They would have bought their teaching, the Torah and many of the scrolls with them. The influence the Jewish captives had on the Babylonian culture, meant Hebrew prophecy was accepted.

The wise men were looking for the coming Messiah, just as Anna prophesied to those in the temple who looked for the redemption in Jerusalem (Luke 2:38). The wise men were more than gentiles or foreigners, because they came to worship the 'King of the Jews'. Not just any king, but their expected, anticipated Messiah, for they had been watching and recognised His star.

To understand the wise men better, and the area they came from, one could assume they were similar to the Samaritans whom the Jews would have nothing to do with (John 4:9b). Having married outside the Jewish culture, they would no longer be considered Jews by those living in Israel. They were not considered covenant people. Jesus told His disciples not to go to the Samaritans (Matt. 10:5). When Jesus did spend time with the Samaritans, they readily accepted every word He said. They too were looking for the Messiah (John 4:1-42). These devout men, unlike the temple shepherds, worshipped Jesus. They selected special gifts suitable to pay homage to the newly-born King.

The Wise Men knew astronomy not astrology. When they headed off to follow the star, it seems from Scripture that the star was no longer apparent in the night sky. Therefore, they went in the general direction of the star they had seen and headed for the palace in Jerusalem. What a surprise when arriving at their destination, nobody knew anything about a newly-born king, especially one born to be 'King of the Jews'. When Herod was told some men were inquiring about a

'King of the Jews', the Bible tells us, *"he was troubled, and all Jerusalem with him"* (Matt. 2:3). As these non-Jewish people gave allegiance to the Emperor and Rome, the announcement of a new 'King of the Jews', threatened their very existence. Herod was disturbed and summonsed the Priests and asked them what they knew.

It had been about fifteen months since the birth of Jesus. Some young temple priests who were shepherds at the time, minding the unblemished lambs, remembered the night well. When they shared the news of their experience in Bethlehem, those who knew the scripture, were able to interpret the Old Testament writings. The priests conveyed the findings to Herod, the reigning king.

Herod summoned the Eastern Wise Men and told them to go to Bethlehem. It would be in this insignificant small town; they would find the King they were looking for. Being an evil king, he sought to destroy anyone who would or could be an obstacle to him and his allegiance to Rome, so he told the Wise Men to return and tell him about the location of the king, so he could also go and worship.

The Wise Men left Herod's presence and once again began their long journey to find the elusive King. While they thought they were about to end their journey, the Holy Spirit was not done with them yet. To their surprise and delight, the star they had seen some fifteen months previously, stood before them, and they were overjoyed at the sight being revealed to them again. The star led them away from Jerusalem and northward to Nazareth. They obediently followed the star, no longer relying on their own initiative.

The Wise Men left Herod thinking they were travelling to Bethlehem, only a short distance away. The Bible tells us, *"And behold, the star which they had seen in the east, reappeared and went before them, till it came and stood over where the young child was. When they saw the reappearance of the star, they rejoiced with exceeding great joy"* (Matt. 2:9b).

We need to consider the implications of, *"And behold, the star which they had seen in the east, reappeared and went before them"* (Matt. 2:9b). The Wise Men are following a star and have no idea where the star was taking them. If the journey was about three days on a donkey, how long did it take them on their mode of transport? They just faithfully followed the star. They had no idea where they were going and how long it would take. Does this say something to us about walking in faith, as we follow and carry out God's directions for us, without questioning?

The Wise Men followed the star which stood over Mary and Joseph's home, marking the place where they would find the One born to be 'King of the Jews'. The Wise Men ventured inside, and found the young boy Jesus, a child in His second year. They knelt before Him and worshipped Him, then offered their gifts of Gold, Frankincense, and Myrrh to Him. Satisfied they had completed their journey and fulfilled their purpose, they rested. An Angel appeared as they rested and warned them not to return to Jerusalem and Herod, but to go back to their own country another way. As they were wise men, Herod's plan was obvious, so they were obedient to the command of God.

When the shepherds were in the field watching their sheep, an angel of the Lord *'stood'* before them. (Luke 2:9a).

We read that the star *'stood'* over the home of Joseph and Mary (Matt. 2:9). Was it really a star that *'stood'* over where the young child was or was it an angel?

When Herod realised the Wise Men had ignored his instructions, and were not returning to report the child's whereabouts, he enquired again of the priests, about the date of the child's birth. When Herod realised it was some sixteen months previous, he realised the census was being carried out. He had all the required information he needed. By checking the registration of each person, the address would be known to him. He commanded all boys under two years of age to be killed. This was only a local directive, and would have only affected a few families, but Herod would have his revenge, as he was accustomed to being obeyed.

But God was in control, and His promise to Mary still stood with regard to protection, the Holy Spirit warned Joseph to take his family and go to Egypt and to stay there until they were told it was safe to return. Joseph obeyed the angel's instructions, and they packed up what they needed and travelled to Egypt. God's protection went with them, even as they went through Jerusalem to get to Egypt. When Joseph, Mary and Jesus arrived at Egypt, they settled into a new home and environment.

The Holy Spirit was certainly embracing Mary and her husband Joseph as the angel promised that the power of the Highest would overshadow them. Obeying the prompting of the Holy Spirit to travel to Egypt, would be a complete act of trust. God always shows up when needed, and this was no exception. They now had the necessary finance to make the dangerous trip, through Jerusalem where Herod was, to Egypt and set up home once again. Now it was all about trust in God to provide and protect, until the time was safe for them to return home to family and friends.

An Allegory: From the Cradle to the Grave.

Luke's gospel recounts the shepherds' angelic encounter. *Now there were in the same country shepherds living out in the fields, keeping watch over their flock by night. And behold, an angel of the Lord stood before them, and the glory of the Lord shone around them, and they were greatly afraid. Then the angel said to them, "Do not be afraid, for behold, I bring you good tidings of great joy which will be to all people. For there is born to you this day in the city of David a Saviour, who is Christ the Lord. And this will be the sign to you: You will find a Babe wrapped in swaddling clothes, lying in a manger." And suddenly there was with the angel a multitude of the heavenly host praising God and saying: "Glory to God in the highest, and on earth peace, goodwill toward men!" So, it was, when the angels had gone away from them into heaven, that the shepherds said to one another, "Let us now go to Bethlehem and see this thing that has come to pass, which the Lord has made known to us." And they came with haste and found Mary and Joseph, and the Babe lying in a manger. Now when they had seen Him, they made widely known the saying which was told them concerning this Child. And all those who heard it marvelled at those things which were told them by the shepherds. But Mary kept all these things and pondered them in her heart. Then the shepherds returned, glorifying and praising God for all the things that they had heard and seen, as it was told them*. (Luke 2:8-20)

Let me share a story with you about the night Jesus was born and His sacrifice for us.

The Setting

The sheep pens were probably made of stones piled on top of each other, with thorny vines over the outside and top, to keep away any predators. An opening in each would provide a place where the shepherd could sit, acting as a gate to keep the sheep and lambs inside. A fire would be burning, not too far from the shepherd to keep each of the shepherds warm and those walking the circumference of these pens, for when they returned.

The Shepherd Cast

Aaron: "Exalted one." *Enoch*: "Dedicated." *Hiram*:" Exalted brother." *Hosea*: "Salvation." *Ira*: "Watchful." *Jordan*: "To flow down" or "descend." *Levi*: "Joining" or "adhering." *Nathan*: "Gift." *Noah*: "Rest" or "comfort." *Reuben*: "Behold, a son." *Seth*: "Appointed." *Solomon*: "Peaceful."

The Story Retold

A number of trainee priests were watching the unblemished lambs and sheep, that would be used in the temple sacrifices. The trainees were Aaron, Enoch, Hiram, Hosea, Ira, Jordan, Levi, Nathan, Noah, Rueben, Seth and Solomon. It was a beautiful clear night and two of the young shepherds were talking to pass the time during the long hours of the night.

'Not much happening tonight, Ira,' said Enoch.

'Not quite so, my brother. I have noticed a glow in the night sky that is very unusual,' replied Ira.

Having heard the conversation, Jordan, Levi and Nathan joined them. All of a sudden, out of nowhere, an angel of the Lord stood before them. A light shone from the heavenly being, and the glory of the Lord encompassed them all. The young shepherds were so afraid, they huddled together in a bunch on the ground.

It was then the angel spoke to them, *"Do not be afraid, for behold, I bring you good tidings of great joy which will be for all people. For there is born to you this day in the city of David a Saviour, who is Christ the Lord. And this will be the sign to you. You will find a Babe wrapped in swaddling clothes, lying in a manger."*

The young men were awe-struck lifting their heads cautiously to view what was happening. Then a great choir, a multitude of the heavenly hosts joined the angel, who filled the night sky. They were praising God and singing,

"Glory to God in the highest, and on earth peace, goodwill toward men!"

And then the angelic beings were gone. Everything returned to quiet. Not even the sheep had stirred.

"I don't know about the rest of you, but I have never experienced anything like that before in my life," said Seth.

"Everything is so peaceful and quite now. Did you notice the sheep and lambs did not move? They were not at all scared," said Solomon.

"I would like to go and see the Baby that the angel told us about. Anyone else interested?" said Nathan.

"Well, we can't all go. How about Jordan and myself watch the sheep and lambs? They are content just sitting in their sheepfolds, and the rest of you go," said Levi.

And so, it was agreed. Away the young shepherds went, talking amongst themselves about all they had seen, heard and happened as they hurried to Bethlehem.

It wasn't a long journey from the grazing areas and the sheepfolds to Bethlehem. As they moved quickly along the road and through the narrow streets, suddenly Ira said, "Look! There's a light and some noise coming from that house. Let's try there." Sure enough, they found a newly-born

Baby wrapped in swaddling cloths, lying in a manger, with His parents, Mary and Joseph next to Him, just as the angel had said.

Mary and Joseph, and the other family members were stunned that the shepherds would come to their home during the night. The young shepherds, full of excitement were eager to tell what had happened to them, what the angel had said, and how the heavenly hosts sang. The family members were totally amazed to hear this had taken place only a little distance from their family home, as they had not seen or heard a thing.

Mary's response was different. She sat quietly, taking in everything she heard. She would long remember the events of this evening.

So much had happened that night; the many family members struggled to come to terms with all they had been told.

The shepherds on the other hand, were praising God as they bid the family farewell and made their way back to their sheep and lambs and the other shepherds. As they left, the shepherds told all the villagers about what they had seen and experienced during the night.

This now poses a question, 'Where did the Wise Men worship Jesus, the child?' You would remember, eight days after the baby was born, He was circumcised (Luke 2:21). After the 40-day purification time for Mary was completed, they went to Jerusalem, to present Him to the Lord (Luke 2:22-24). Jesus, having been born on Passover, fifty days later would make this the second must-attend feast, that being the 'Feast of Weeks' or as we call it, "Pentecost" (Luke 2:25-38). After presenting Jesus at the Temple during the Feast of Weeks, my Bible tells me, *"So when they had performed all things according to the law of the Lord, they returned to Galilee, to their own city, Nazareth"* (Luke 2:39).

We are not told there were actually Three Wise Men, but because three gifts were given, this has suggested the use of three. Another accepted belief is that the Star guided these men to where Jesus was born. While the Wise Men saw and recognised a star or sign in the east, the star did not lead them in their journey to Jerusalem. They knew the direction and headed toward what they had seen. Reasoning would suggest a King be born in a palace, but not this time.

Some time passed. The young shepherds had finished their training as shepherds and had taken their place in the temple, joining the senior Temple Priests. Then came an occasion when they were all called, to be questioned by the High Priest. Apparently, Herod, the reigning Jewish puppet king, was asking about a baby who was born to be the King of the Jews. He had it on good authority, that some Wise Men from the east had seen His star, which signified the birth of a future King for the Jews, and they had travelled to his palace, where they naturally thought the baby would be. Herod needed some answers and he wanted them now!

As the young priests looked at each other in amazement, they remembered only too well the events of the night in Bethlehem when they were minding the temple lambs.

It was Seth who spoke up saying, *"In Bethlehem of Judea, for thus it is written by the prophet, 'But you, Bethlehem, in the land of Judea, are not the least among the rulers of Judah; for out of you shall come a Ruler Who will shepherd My people Israel'."* Herod was pleased with this information and returned to tell the Wise Men. The one born destined to be King of the Jews could be found in Bethlehem. Herod was a cunning king. He had not risen to power by good means. He told the Wise Men, that when they had searched and found the One, to tell him where He was living, so he could also go and worship Him. The Wise Men hearing what King Herod had said, bid him farewell, and left to continue seeking this elusive King of the Jews.

I would draw your attention to a verse of scripture that says, *"When they saw the star, they were filled with exceedingly great joy"* (Matt. 2:10). The star the Wise Men had seen previously, back in their country, now reappeared. My Bible says, *"When they heard the king, they departed; and behold, the star which they had seen in the East went before them, till it came and stood over where the young child was"* (Matt. 2:9). The wise men had been given wrong information as to the whereabouts of *'He, who is born King of the Jews'* (Matt. 2:2a). They were told He was born in Bethlehem, but the star was leading them to Nazareth.

Jesus was now living as a Child in Nazareth, and this is why, *"The star, which they had first seen in the East, went before them, till it came and stood over where the young Child was"* (Matt. 2:9). At the reappearance of the star they had seen previously, they were exceedingly joyful.

Being Wise Men, they knew what to do, and rather than listen to what King Herod had told them, they followed the heavenly manifestation. God now led them the last part of the journey. The Wise Men now saw Jesus the child, not a baby, and presented Him with their gifts. No Wise Men at the manger scene.

Back in Jerusalem, Herod was becoming anxious. 'Where were these so-called Wise Men', he thought. He recalled the priest who had told him about the prophecy that the babe would be born in Bethlehem. Herod then gave orders to his soldiers to kill all the young boys two years and under in Bethlehem, which they did. There would have been very few boys in Bethlehem, as this was the least of all the towns. How could Herod be sure he had eliminated this one who would have opposed his kingdom? Having recalled the priest who had freely given him the earlier information, he would then know who the family was. You would remember, the Bible tells us, when the shepherds had found the Baby, His parents, Mary and Joseph were with Him (Luke 2:16).

The angel had told Mary previously, that she would be overshadowed, and protected by the God of the Highest. The Wise Men, having been divinely warned in a dream, they should not return to Herod, departed for their own country, returning another way. Joseph also had a dream, warning him about the impending doom. Along with Mary and Jesus, they fled to Egypt where they stayed until Herod died. Matthew 2:19 to 23, speaks about the time when Joseph, the young Child and His mother returned to Nazareth. Herod was dead. There was now nothing to fear.

There is a time coming when we will be called to our new home. All the evil forces will be imprisoned for eternity along with all the fallen angels and those who have not accepted Jesus Christ as their Lord and Saviour.

While this is the end of the shepherds and wise men's role, Herod still had a part to play. You would remember; he had children. One son succeeded him in governing his kingdom of Judea. His name was Herod Antipas. His father died when

Jesus, with His parents were in Egypt. Herod Antipas reigned from AD 1 to 39. This made him well and truly alive when Jesus was born, and he would have certainly known about the baby born 'King of the Jews' and how his father saw Him as a threat to his throne. Herod Antipas would have also known about the massacre of the children, two years and under, as his father tried his best to rid the nation of this would-be leader.

We pick up the story where Jesus has been arrested in the Garden of Gethsemane and taken before the elders, High Priest and finally, the Sanhedrin. After Jesus had been asked many questions, He was confronted with a question; they all wanted an answer too.

"Jesus, we need a direct answer, 'Are You the Son of God?'" asked Caiaphas the High Priest.

"It is as you say," replied Jesus.

"Blasphemy. We have all heard what He said," yelled Caiaphas, and with this, being so enraged, he, Caiaphas, tore his clothes. By tearing his clothes, Caiaphas had made himself ritually unclean (Lev. 21:10), and could not perform his duties at the Passover, so his father-in-law Annas, was reinstated to officiate that year.

Jesus was bound and led to Pilate. After all the accusations were made, Pilate confronted Jesus with his own question.

"Are You the King of the Jews?" asked Pilate.

"It is as you say," replied Jesus.

Pilate said to the chief priests and the crowd, "I find no fault in Him."

"But He has stirred up people, teaching throughout all Judea, beginning from Galilee to this place," said the chief priest.

"So, You are a Galilean. Why did you bring Him to me priest? This case belongs to Herod. Away with you," said Pilate.

Herod just happened to be in Jerusalem at the time. When the priests brought Jesus to Herod, he was extremely glad to meet Jesus as he had heard a lot about the Man. After Herod had asked Jesus many questions, the chief priests and scribes vehemently accused Jesus, He said nothing. Herod became annoyed with Jesus, and his men of war treated Jesus with contempt, mocking Him, and finally sent Jesus back to Pilate.

Herod and Pilate became friends that day, overcoming the tension that had previously existed between them. Herod Antipas was the son of Herod the Great. He had Jesus' cousin, John the Baptist beheaded at the request of his wife Herodias's daughter, Salome. As he looked at Jesus, did he think to himself, *'You are the one my father feared. My father will have his wish to have you killed, but not by my hands'.* One could imagine Herod and Pilate talking and Herod Antipas sharing with him the things of the past.

"Herod!" said Pilate, with fear in his voice as he considers the possible consequences of his actions.

"Pilate, you sent this Jesus to me for sentencing, did you not?" said Antipas.

"Yes, I did, for He is a Galilean," replied Pilate.

"I remember when growing up, my father tried to kill this man when He was but a child, but all his efforts failed. My father saw Him as a threat to his kingdom's power. As a favour, maybe you could do what my father could not?" suggested Herod.

What was Pilate to do? Appease his new friend Herod and give in to the priest's claim, knowing the priests were envious of Jesus' popularity and also being a threat to their religion.

"Have nothing to do with this just Man, for I have suffered many things today in a dream because of Him," said Pilate's wife.

"Away with you woman! We will talk later," replied Pilate.

Pilate exercised his authority and had a sign placed on the cross, above Jesus' head that read, *"Jesus of Nazareth, the King of the Jews"* in three languages; Hebrew, Greek and Latin. Even the priests wanted Pilate to change the inscription to "He said, 'I am the King of the Jews'." Was Pilate saying to all those who believed, 'Your King is finally dead!' While Herod Antipas and Pilate may have thought His death was the end, actually, it was only the beginning.

It seems to me, what I have written, although not being authenticated, works. While many could find flaws, I am satisfied with the outcome. Having attended two of the 'must-attend feasts', I am looking forward to attending the third when summoned. Pray that the Lord of the harvest will return soon.

Notes

Notes

Other books by the Author

Have you ever searched the four gospels to obtain the full account of Jesus life?

The Author, under their guidance of the Holy Spirit,took the words of the Apostle Paul to heart, when he wrote to Timothy and encouraged him to: "Study to show yourself approved unto God, a workman that needs not be ashamed, rightly dividing the word of truth".
2 Timothy 2:15.

The Life of Jesus A Simple Narrative

In 'The Life of Jesus. A Simple Narrative', the author used language, similar to the New King James Version of the Bible to order and blend the four gospels into one complete story.

The Life of Christ Simply Told

In the Second book, 'The Life of Christ Simply Told', the author used language, similar to the New International Version of the Bible to order and blend the four gospels into the complete story of Jesus life.

Series titles available:

Book One	***The Defiant Mouse***
Book Two	***The Curious Chicken***
Book Three	***A Dog in Need***
Book Four	***An Old Friend Found***
Book Five	***The Rescue***
Book Six	***The Bush Fire***
Book Seven	***A Bad Influence***
Book Eight	***A Shining Light***
Book Nine	***Hidden Secrets***
Book Ten	***A Foiled Plot***
Book Eleven	***Running the Race***
Book Twelve	***An Unexpected Reward***
Book Thirteen	***Max Meets a Friend***
Book Fourteen	***Reflections***

Books available from *The Adventures of Max* Facebook page, and www.wittonbooks.com